dream whip
no. 14

dream whip
no. 14
by
bill brown

write to:
p.o. box 53832
lubbock, tx.
79453
dreamwhip @ gmail.com

ISBN # 0-9770557-8-7
microcosm # 76044
microcosm publishing
p.o. box 14332
portland, or. 97293
www. microcosmpublishing. com

Issue XIV:
THE HOMELAND SECURITY ISSUE.

THERE ARE TRAIN STORIES AND BUS STORIES, AND THERE'S EVEN A STORY ABOUT TAKING A BOAT TO GERMANY THAT SOMEHOW TURNS INTO A STORY ABOUT MOVING TO DETROIT.

THE HOLY LAND EXPERIENCE

TO GET TO THE HOLY LAND, TAKE INTERSTATE 4 TO ORLANDO, FLORIDA AND GET OFF AT EXIT 78. YOU CAN'T MISS IT. IT'S THE PLACE THAT LOOKS LIKE JERUSALEM. I PULL UP TO THE FRONT GATE. A GUARD TAKES A LOOK IN THE BACK OF MY PICK-UP TRUCK. I WONDER IF HE'S REALLY CHECKING FOR A BOMB, OR IF HE'S JUST AN ACTOR PRETENDING TO CHECK FOR A BOMB. EITHER WAY, IT ADDS TO THE AUTHENTICITY OF THE PLACE. I MEAN, WHAT KIND OF HOLY LAND THEME PARK WOULD THIS BE WITHOUT AT LEAST THE SUGGESTION OF SUICIDE BOMBERS? I PARK AT THE FAR END OF THE PARKING LOT, NEXT TO A ROW OF CHURCH BUSES FROM CHURCHES

ALL OVER THE SOUTH : ABYSSINIAN
BAPTIST CHURCH ; TENNILE CHURCH
OF CHRIST; GOOD SHEPHERD A.M.E.
I SHELL OUT 20 BUCKS FOR A
TICKET (GIVE UNTO CAESAR WHAT
IS CAESAR'S, INDEED) AND PASS
THROUGH A HIGH-TECH, COMPUTER-
IZED TURNSTILE. AND SUDDENLY,
IT'S 2000 YEARS AGO. SORT OF.
IT'S A PAST THAT'S BEEN
INFILTRATED BY THE FUTURE,
WHERE BEARDED PHARISEES AND
ROMAN CENTURIONS SHOULDER
PAST SUNBURNED TEENAGERS
WEARING FLIP-FLOPS AND FLORIDA
GATORS T-SHIRTS.
I CHECK MY GLOSSY HOLY LAND
EXPERIENCE MAP TO SEE WHERE I
SHOULD GO. THERE'S THE
WILDERNESS TABERNACLE, WHERE
"A HIGH PRIEST GUIDES YOU ON
A TOUR OF THE ANCIENT

SACRIFICIAL SYSTEM. " OVER AT
THE THEATER OF LIFE, THERE'S A
"25 - MINUTE, MULTI - SENSORY FILM
THAT POWERFULLY COMMUNICATES
GOD'S MASTER PLAN FOR
REDEEMING MANKIND " (THE
BROCHURE NOTES THAT PARENTAL
DISCRETION IS ADVISED "DUE TO
THE REALISM OF THE CRUCIFIXION
SCENE "). I OPT FOR THE
JERUSALEM MODEL A.D. 66. IT'S
A ROOM - SIZED MODEL OF OLD
JERUSALEM THAT'S ALOT LIKE
THE MODEL OF NEW YORK CITY AT
THE QUEENS MUSEUM THAT WAS
BUILT FOR THE 1939 WORLD'S
FAIR, ONLY THIS MODEL HAS
MINIATURE ROMAN SOLDIERS
MARCHING PAST SHEPHERDS TENDING
MINIATURE SHEEP. A HIPPY DUDE
STANDING NEXT TO ME IS

INFORMING ONE OF THE DOCENTS THAT IT'S NOT JUST CHRISTIANS WHO FEEL LIKE WE'RE LIVING IN THE END TIMES, BUT BUDDHISTS AND HINDUS FEEL THE SAME WAY. LATER, THIS SAME DOCENT CLIMBS ON TOP OF THE MODEL LIKE SOME PAGAN COLOSSUS AND SHINES A RED LASER POINTER AT THE IMPORTANT BUILDINGS. HE ZAPS KING HEROD'S PALACE, AND THE LAST SUPPER BUILDING, AND THE BUILDING WHERE PONTIUS PILATE GAVE THE CROWD A CHOICE BETWEEN JESUS AND BARABUS, AND OF COURSE EVERYONE VOTED FOR BARABUS. IF JESUS CAME BACK TODAY AND WOUND UP ON SOME TV SHOW LIKE "AMERICAN IDOL," HE'D STILL LOSE OUT TO BARABUS. THAT'S THE THING ABOUT US HUMAN BEINGS. WE LOVE THE BAD BOYS.

THE DOCENT WITH THE LASER
POINTER GIVES A LITTLE SPEECH
ABOUT PONTIUS PILATE. IT'S
PRETTY CLEAR HE DOESN'T HAVE
MUCH SYMPATHY FOR THE GUY.
BUT IT SEEMS TO ME WE SHOULD
CUT PILATE A LITTLE SLACK.
YEAH, HE WAS PROBABLY AN
ARROGANT THUG, BUT HERE HE
WAS, A ROMAN COP TRYING TO
KEEP THE LID ON A CITY FULL
OF RELIGIOUS FANATICS WHO
HATED HIS GUTS. PLUS, HE HAD
THE MISFORTUNE TO BE THE GUY
WHO CONDEMNED THE SON OF
GOD ALMIGHTY TO A GRISLY
DEATH, WHICH DEFINITELY ISN'T
SOMETHING THAT'S EASY TO
LIVE DOWN.
BACK OUTSIDE, ON THE QUMRAN
CAVE STAGE, A BALDING JESUS
WITH A HEADSET MICROPHONE IS
GIVING A SERMON. HE URGES THE

CROWD OF SWEATING CHURCH GROUPS,
AND OLD FOLKS IN BASEBALL CAPS,
AND TEENAGERS WHO ARE
SEETHING INSIDE BECAUSE WHEN
MOM AND DAD SAID THEY WERE
GOING TO A THEME PARK IN ORLANDO,
FLORIDA, THIS ISN'T THE ONE
THEY HAD IN MIND, TO MOVE
FORWARD AND GATHER AROUND.
"COME CLOSE, MY CHILDREN, "
THE FAKE JESUS SAYS. THEN
HE CHORTLES. I GUESS HE
FIGURES THAT'S WHAT THE REAL
JESUS WOULD HAVE DONE AT THE
SIGHT OF HIS DISCIPLES. BUT
WHEREAS THE REAL JESUS'
CHORTLE PROBABLY SOUNDED
SINCERE, THE FAKE JESUS'
CHORTLE SOUNDS FORCED AND A
LITTLE SINISTER. A 2-YEAR-OLD
GIRL NEAR ME STARTS TO CRY,
AND I THINK I RECOGNIZE IN

HER THE SAME TERROR I FELT THE FIRST TIME I FOUND MYSELF ON THE LAP OF A FAKE SANTA CLAUS AT THE MALL. IT'S THE TERROR YOU FEEL WHEN YOU FIRST REALIZE THERE'S A BIG DIFFERENCE BETWEEN SOMEONE WHO LOVES YOU AND SOMEONE WHO'S JUST ACTING LIKE THEY DO.

The first gulf war of 1991, which kicked off the cable-news mini-series form, pioneered this sort of hype, but the coverage of the current war has taken it to a new level. "The characters are the same: the president is a Bush, and the other guy is Hussein," Erik Sorenson, president of MSNBC, told USA Today. "But the technology — the military's and the media's — has exploded." He likened the change to "the difference between Atari and PlayStation," and added that "this may be one time where the sequel is more compelling than the original."

Columbus, Mississippi

HANS CHRISTIAN ANDERSEN WORRIED
ABOUT BEING BURIED ALIVE. THE
SAME GUY WHO WROTE "THE UGLY
DUCKLING" AND "THE LITTLE
MERMAID," NOT TO MENTION
"THE PRINCESS AND THE PEA,"
WOULD LEAVE A NOTE BY HIS
BED EVERY NIGHT BEFORE HE
WENT TO SLEEP THAT SAID
"I ONLY APPEAR TO BE DEAD."
IT'S ONLY A GUESS, BUT I BET HE
STARTED DOING THIS AFTER SOME
CARELESS COMMENT BY A FRIEND.
"GEE, HANS, YOU SURE ARE A DEEP
SLEEPER," THE FRIEND MAY HAVE
SAID. "IT'S LIKE YOU'RE DEAD."
WHEN YOU'RE NEUROTIC, A
COMMENT SUCH AS THIS IS LIKE
A SEED, THAT EVENTUALLY SPROUTS
AND GROWS INTO A GREAT BIG

PHOBIA. TRUST ME. I KNOW. THEN
AGAIN, MAYBE HANS CHRISTIAN
ANDERSEN WAS RIGHT TO WORRY.
BACK IN THE 19TH CENTURY,
BEING BURIED ALIVE WASN'T
UNHEARD OF. I ONCE VISITED A
CEMETERY IN BERLIN WHERE
SOME OF THE GRAVES HAD
SPEAKING TUBES, STICKING OUT
OF THE GROUND LIKE LITTLE
PERISCOPES. THE IDEA WAS
THAT IF YOU'D BEEN INADVERT-
ENTLY PLANTED IN THE GROUND,
YOU COULD SHOUT INTO THE
TUBE FOR HELP. NOWADAYS,
PEOPLE DON'T WORRY TOO MUCH
ABOUT BEING BURIED ALIVE. WHEN
I THINK ABOUT IT, I'M NOT
SURE WHY WE SHOULD ALL FEEL
SO CONFIDENT THAT SOME
UNDER-TRAINED ASSISTANT
MORTICIAN WILL NOTICE, OR

EVEN CARE, IF WE'RE JUST EVER-
SO-SLIGHTLY STILL ALIVE.
MAYBE FEARS HAVE THEIR
FASHIONS, AND BEING BURIED
ALIVE, LIKE WEARING A CORSET
OR A CRAVAT, IS JUST OUT
OF STYLE.
ALL OF WHICH CONSTITUTES A
CONVERSATION I WAS HAVING ONE
NIGHT IN COLUMBUS, MISSISSIPPI
WITH MY FRIEND, JOHNNY. JOHNNY
GOES TO SCHOOL IN COLUMBUS. HE
TELLS ME IT'S A VERY PROPER
LITTLE SOUTHERN TOWN THAT
JUST HAPPENS TO BE FULL OF
ODDBALLS. LIKE MOTHER GOOSE,
FOR INSTANCE: AN OLDER LADY
WHO WEARS A LONG SKIRT AND A
FLOPPY SUNBONNET, AND WHO
STORMS INTO LOCAL RESTAURANTS
AND SINGS NURSERY RHYMES
TILL SOMEONE KICKS HER OUT.
THEN THERE'S THE OLD MAN WHO

DRIVES AROUND TOWN WITH A
TRAILER FULL OF OLD BARBIE DOLLS,
AND THERE'S THE REALLY OLD
MAN WHO PLAYS A GUITAR ON
THE STREET AND MAKES UP SONGS
WITH FILTHY LYRICS.

JOHNNY TAKES ME OVER TO THE
WOMEN'S COLLEGE WHERE HE'S
DIRECTING A PLAY. NEXT TO THE
THEATER DEPARTMENT IS A HUGE
PILE OF DEBRIS THAT USED TO BE
THE GYM BUILDING BEFORE A
TORNADO SLAMMED INTO IT LAST
OCTOBER. THE TORNADO ALSO
SLICED THE TOP OFF THE ART
BUILDING, THEN SLIPPED INTO
SOME PASSING STORM CLOUD AND
MADE A CLEAN GETAWAY.
JOHNNY TELLS ME A SECOND
TORNADO HIT THE LOCAL BEER
DISTRIBUTOR'S WAREHOUSE. IT
TORE THE BUILDING AWAY,

LEAVING BEHIND HUNDREDS OF
NEATLY STACKED CASES OF
BEER. FOR WEEKS AFTER THE
TORNADO HIT, GARBAGE CANS
AND RECYCLING BINS ALL OVER
TOWN WERE FULL OF EMPTY
CANS OF LOOTED BUD LITE.

A FEW DAYS LATER, I DRIVE
ACROSS ALABAMA, FOLLOWING
THE PATH OF A RECENT STORM.
THERE'S A LOT OF DAMAGE : TREES
AND TELEPHONE POLES SNAPPED
IN HALF, AND HOUSES WITH
BIG BLUE TARPS COVERING THE
HOLES IN THEIR ROOFS. THE
STORM DAMAGE MAKES ALL THE
LITTLE TOWNS I PASS THROUGH
SEEM SHAKY AND UNSURE. IN
FACT, NOT JUST THESE LITTLE
TOWNS, BUT AMERICA, TOO. THE
WHOLE PLACE. A COUNTRY BUILT

ON FAULT LINES AND FLOOD PLAINS AND IN THE PATH OF TORNADOES. IT ALL SEEMS IFFY.

IN MONTGOMERY, THE WEATHER GETS SCARY SO I STOP AT A MOTEL FOR THE NIGHT. AROUND 4 AM, I WAKE UP TO SOMETHING TAPPING ON MY WINDOW. HAIL. I SWITCH ON THE TV AND FIND A LOCAL STATION THAT'S BROADCASTING A LIVE IMAGE OF A WEATHER RADAR SCREEN. A CLOUD OF ANGRY RED PIXELS SEEMS TO BE BEARING DOWN ON THE CITY, BUT BECAUSE THERE'S NO WEATHER REPORTER TO EXPLAIN THINGS, IT'S HARD TO TELL WHAT'S GOING ON. THERE'S JUST THIS RADAR IMAGE, AND IN THE BACKGROUND THERE'S THE SOUNDTRACK MUSIC FROM THE MOVIE THE PERFECT

STORM. I OPEN MY DOOR. IN THE DISTANCE, I CAN HEAR TORNADO SIRENS. BACK HOME IN TEXAS, THE TORNADO SIRENS ARE AIR RAID SIRENS, COLD WAR-ERA RELICS THAT SOUND LIKE GHOST DOGS HOWLING AT THE MOON. HERE IN MONT-GOMERY, THE SIRENS HAVE BEEN UPDATED. THEY'RE HIGH-PITCHED AND STEADY. THE SOUND OF TERROR DISTILLED INTO AN ELECTRONIC TONE. IF THOSE OLD-FASHIONED SIRENS MARKED THE END OF THE WORLD WITH A MOURNFUL ANALOG WAIL, THESE NEW SIRENS MARK IT WITH A PIERCING DIGITAL SHRIEK.

ON THE TV, A WEATHERMAN SUDDENLY APPEARS. HE'S GOT BAGS UNDER HIS EYES AND STUBBLE ON HIS CHIN. HE

REPORTS THAT A TORNADO HAS
BEEN SPOTTED NEAR ECLECTIC,
ALABAMA. IT FIGURES.
TORNADOES ARE ALWAYS ON
THE LOOK-OUT FOR TOWNS
WITH QUIRKY NAMES. I GUESS
IT KEEPS THEIR JOB OF RANDOM
DESTRUCTION INTERESTING. A
COUPLE YEARS AGO, A TORNADO
SMASHED THROUGH A TOWN NOT
FAR FROM WHERE I GREW UP
CALLED HAPPY, TEXAS. "THE
TOWN WITHOUT A FROWN," IT
CALLS ITSELF. WHEN YOU'RE A
TORNADO, HOW CAN YOU RESIST
A TOWN WITH A NAME LIKE
THAT?

I SWITCH THE TV CHANNEL TO
CNN. THERE'S A LIVE FEED
FROM BAGHDAD, AND THERE
ARE AIR RAID SIRENS SOUNDING

THERE, TOO. THE OLD-FASHIONED KIND. IT'S APRIL, 2003, AND IT'S NOT A TORNADO THAT'S MOVING IN, BUT THE U.S. MARINES. THE THUNDER AND THE TORNADO SIRENS OUTSIDE MY MOTEL ROOM MIX WITH THE AIR RAID SIRENS AND THE ANTI-AIRCRAFT FIRE COMING FROM THE TV. I TURN OFF THE TV AND TAKE COVER IN THE BATHTUB AND WAIT FOR THE STORM TO PASS.

ave you ever found yourself wide-awake at 2 o'clock in the morning? You're restless and your mind won't stop; all sorts of thoughts and ideas keep running through your mind. On one such night in February 1966, Cleve Backster, Chairman of the Research and Instrumentation Committee of the American Polygraph Association, was preparing for a six-week course at his School of Lie Detection in New York City.

Finishing up well past midnight, he noticed his plants needed watering. In this fertile late-night state, he began to wonder how long it would take for the water to go from the roots of the plants to the leaves. Backster wondered whether his polygraph, commonly known as a lie detector, if connected to a leaf, would register a straight, upward line indicating the arrival of water.

PLANT CONNECTED TO POLYGRAPH

So after watering his dracaena, he connected the polygraph to one of the plant's leaves.

Backster watched not knowing what would happen. The paper began to move and record. However, the line did not go straight upward as he expected, instead it showed a downward trend with a series of little spikes.

Astonished that the recording did not trend upward, he mused on what might affect the plant. Inquisitive by nature, Backster decided to threaten the plant's well being. First he decided to dunk one of the leaves in his cup of coffee. No response. Maybe it wasn't hot enough.

Then the inspiration came to him to get a match and burn a leaf. The instant he had that thought, and before he could act on it, the recording pen made a long upward sweep. Had the electrodes been connected to a human being, this would have indicated an increase in electrical activity and that the person was lying. Could the plant have read his thoughts?

PLANT RESPONDS TO THOUGHT

The next day Backster showed the results of his night's experimentation to his associate. Curious, his associate expressed his desire to also burn a leaf. At the very same instant he had that thought, the polygraph registered an upward surge. However, this time Backster decided he didn't want him to harm the plant.

Interestingly, the plant knew they weren't going to hurt it, and were only pretending. The pen showed no reaction. The plants knew what Backster and his associate were thinking; the plants were able to read their thoughts. As a result of an article on his research in the April 1969 issue of "Electro Technology," Backster's discovery came to be known as "The Backster Effect."

NEW ORLEANS.

ST. ROCH IS THE PATRON SAINT OF
LOST CAUSES. HE'S A GOOD PATRON
SAINT FOR NEW ORLEANS WHICH,
EVEN BEFORE THE HURRICANE, WAS
A TOWN OF LOST CAUSES. THERE'S
A CEMETERY DEDICATED TO ST.
ROCH IN THE MARIGNY DISTRICT.
THE STORY GOES THAT ST. ROCH
MINISTERED TO PLAGUE VICTIMS IN
ITALY DURING THOSE DARK DAYS
WHEN EVERYONE WAS DYING OF IT.
THEN HE GOT THE PLAGUE, TOO, AND
WANDERED OFF INTO THE WOODS TO
DIE. BUT THEN A LITTLE DOG
SHOWED UP AND KEPT BRINGING HIM
FOOD, WHICH IS A CUTE STORY, BUT
A LITTLE DISTURBING, TOO. I MEAN,
WHERE WAS THE DOG GETTING THIS
FOOD, AND WHAT KIND OF FOOD
WAS IT? IT'S BEEN MY EXPERIENCE
THAT DOGS AREN'T EXACTLY

DISCRIMINATING ABOUT WHAT THEY
CONSIDER FOOD. NEVERTHELESS, ST.
ROCH GOT BETTER. MY PAL HELEN
LIVES IN NEW ORLEANS, AND SHE
TELLS ME IF YOU WANT TO ASK ST.
ROCH FOR HELP, YOU'RE SUPPOSED
TO FEED A LITTLE DOG, THEN
VISIT ST. ROCH'S CHAPEL TO SAY
A PRAYER. IF ST. ROCH DOESN'T
MAKE YOU FEEL BETTER, AT LEAST
FEEDING A LITTLE DOG WILL.

THE CHAPEL AT ST. ROCH'S CEMETERY
IS A GOTHIC REVIVAL CHURCH THAT
WAS BUILT IN THE 1870'S AFTER
NEW ORLEANS WENT THROUGH A
YELLOW FEVER EPIDEMIC. OVER
THE YEARS, IT BECAME A PILGRIMAGE
SITE FOR PEOPLE WHO WERE SICK
OR CRIPPLED. THE CHAPEL USED
TO BE FILLED WITH DISCARDED
CRUTCHES AND PROSTHETIC LIMBS
AND LEG BRACES. TONS OF THEM,
HUNG FROM THE WALLS AND PILED
ON THE FLOOR. THE DEBRIS LEFT

BEHIND BY PEOPLE WHO'D BEEN
MIRACULOUSLY CURED. AT SOME
POINT, THE CHAPEL GOT CLEANED
UP. I TRY TO IMAGINE THE PERSON
WHO DECIDED TO DO THIS: SOMEONE
CARRYING A BROOM AND A BIG
GARBAGE BAG, AND MUTTERING
SOMETHING ABOUT HOW MIRACLES
SURE MAKE A GOD AWFUL MESS.
IF YOU PEAK INTO A LITTLE
LOCKED ALCOVE NEXT TO THE
ALTAR, YOU'LL SEE ALL THAT'S
LEFT: A FEW CRUTCHES AND CANES,
AND THESE PLASTER CASTS OF
HANDS AND FEET AND EVEN A
CHEST OR TWO HANGING FROM
HOOKS ON THE WALL. HELEN
EXPLAINS THAT WHEN PEOPLE WERE
CURED BY ST. ROCH, THEY'D
BRING IN PLASTER CASTS OF THEIR
FORMERLY DISEASED BODY PARTS:
WITHERED HANDS AND ARTHRITIC
KNEES AND PARALYZED FEET.

THE PLASTER CASTS WERE A WAY
TO SAY THANKS. FOR DAYS, I
CAN'T GET THOSE PLASTER BODY
PARTS OFF MY MIND. I BEGIN
TO WONDER IF THE BODY PARTS
ST. ROCH CURED STAYED STRONG
AND HEALTHY, EVEN AS THE
REST OF THE PERSON WHO WAS
HEALED GREW OLD AND FRAIL.
I MEAN, DID THE CURED BODY
PARTS OUTLAST THE BODY THEY
BELONGED TO?

LATER, I FIND OUT ST. ROCH ISN'T
THE PATRON SAINT OF LOST CAUSES.
APPARENTLY, THAT'S ST. JUDE.

IN FACT, IT'S NOT EXACTLY CLEAR
WHAT ST. ROCH IS THE PATRON
SAINT OF. MOST PEOPLE SAY HE
HANDLES INVALIDS, BUT THERE'S
ALSO DOGS, SKIN RASHES, KNEE
PROBLEMS, AND THE CITY OF
ISTANBUL.

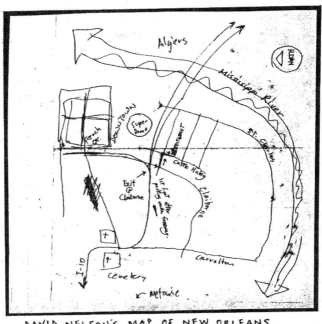

DAVID NELSON'S MAP OF NEW ORLEANS.

DO EUROPEANS STILL APPLAUD WHEN THE PLANE LANDS?

I WAKE UP AT 5AM. I WOULD HAVE GOTTEN UP AT 4 EXCEPT I SLEPT THROUGH THE ALARM. IN FACT, I WOULD GLADLY HAVE DRIVEN STRAIGHT THROUGH THE NIGHT AND STRAIGHT THROUGH TEXAS TOO, BUT THE HIGHWAY LINES WERE STARTING TO BLUR. SO I GOT A ROOM AT A CRUMMY MOTEL IN JASPER, TEXAS. THERE'S DIRTY GRAFFITI CARVED INTO THE TOP OF THE DRESSER, AND A VAST KING-SIZED BED THAT TAKES UP MOST OF THE ROOM. IT'S THE KIND OF BED THAT MIGHT SUGGEST LUXURY AND COMFORT AT SOME 4-STAR HOTEL, BUT HERE, LIT UP BY A NAKED SIXTY-WATT BULB SCREWED INTO THE CEILING, IT JUST SEEMS SAD AND SLEAZY. I CHECK UNDER THE BED FOR BODIES, LIVING OR DEAD, AND I ZIP MYSELF INTO MY SLEEPING BAG. IN THE MORNING, I DRIVE TO AUSTIN AND HEAD

STRAIGHT TO THE FOOD CO-OP. THEN
I ORDER A COUPLE BREAKFAST TACOS:
POTATOES, VEGGIE SAUSAGE, AND
RICE AND BEANS, AND A DOLLOP OF
REALLY HOT SALSA. EVERYTHING
ABOUT AUSTIN SEEMS DIFFERENT AND
EVERYONE I USED TO KNOW HERE HAS
MOVED AWAY, BUT THE BREAKFAST
TACOS ARE EXACTLY THE SAME. AS
IF A LITTLE BIT OF THE YEAR I LIVED
IN THIS TOWN IS STILL HERE, OVER-
LOOKED AND UNDISTURBED, HIDDEN
SAFELY IN THE RECIPE FOR BREAKFAST
TACOS AT THE FOOD CO-OP. I EAT
THE TACOS OUT ON THE PATIO, FEEL-
ING A LITTLE SAD BECAUSE THE PAST
IS A PLACE YOU JUST KEEP GETTING
FARTHER AWAY FROM. AND ANYWAY,
ONE DAY THEY'LL CHANGE THE
TACO RECIPE, AND AUSTIN WILL
BECOME JUST ANOTHER STRANGE
TOWN THAT I'M A STRANGER IN.
AFTER BREAKFAST, I DRIVE ONTO
A HIGHWAY CALLED MOPAC, WHICH
IS SHORT FOR MISSOURI PACIFIC.
THAT'S THE NAME OF THE RAILROAD

THAT THE HIGHWAY'S BUILT NEXT TO. AS I ZIP OVER THE COLORADO RIVER, I CATCH SIGHT OF AUSTIN'S LITTLE SKYLINE, ITS COLLECTION OF GLASS BOXES FROM THE 80'S AND 90'S. IT TAKES ME OFF GUARD, LIKE SEEING AN OLD GIRLFRIEND OR AN OLD BOYFRIEND AFTER A REALLY LONG TIME; SOMEONE YOU HAVEN'T THOUGHT MUCH ABOUT, BUT WHEN YOU SEE THEM, IT ALL COMES BACK TO YOU. THE WAY YOU USED TO FEEL. THE WAY YOU DON'T FEEL ANYMORE.

I DRIVE ALL DAY, ACROSS TEXAS AND MOST OF NEW MEXICO. IN DEMING, I GET A CUP OF COFFEE AND DECIDE TO DRIVE ALL THE WAY TO TUCSON. BUT 60 MILES LATER, IN LORDSBURG, I GIVE UP. INSTEAD, I GET A ROOM AT THE HOLIDAY MOTEL. I'VE STAYED HERE BEFORE, RIGHT ACROSS THE STREET FROM THE SOUTHERN PACIFIC MAINLINE. IT'S MYSTERIOUS, THAT MOTEL, AND NOT JUST BECAUSE OF THE PINE GREEN

NEON TUBES THAT LINE THE EAVES, OF THE OLD SIGN THAT ADVERTISES ROOMS WITH "REFRIGERATED AIR" AND "SAFE HEAT." THE MYSTERIOUS THING IS THE INDOOR POOL IN THE PARKING LOT. THE POOL IS WAY TOO GRAND AND OVERSIZED FOR THE MOTEL, WHICH IS A STANDARD ISSUE CHEAP MOTEL ON THE OLD HIGHWAY THROUGH TOWN. A MOTEL THAT'S BEEN BYPASSED BY THE FREEWAY AND LEFT TO FEND FOR ITSELF WHILE THE CHAIN MOTELS BY THE EXIT RAMP GET ALL THE BUSINESS. TO SURVIVE, A BYPASSED MOTEL HAS TO ADAPT. IT HAS TO INSTALL BULLETPROOF GLASS IN THE LOBBY, AND OFFER ROOMS BY THE WEEK AND BY THE HOUR. IT HAS TO DISPENSE WITH ALL THE AMENITIES: BATH MATS PRINTED WITH THE NAME OF THE MOTEL, AND IN-ROOM COFFEE MAKERS, AND TOILETS SEALED FOR YOUR PROTECTION WITH A PAPER STRIP. EVEN THE VIBRATING BEDS HAVE TO GO — TOO MUCH MAINTENANCE — REPLACED BY

A PORNO CHANNEL ON THE TV. SO IT DOESN'T MAKE SENSE, THIS INDOOR POOL THAT YOU CAN STILL TAKE A SWIM IN. LAST TIME I STAYED AT THE HOLIDAY MOTEL, I TOOK A SWIM. IT WAS A LATE AFTERNOON IN AUGUST, AND I WAS ALL ALONE, FLOATING IN THE POOL WHILE FREIGHT TRAINS RUMBLED BY ACROSS THE STREET. THE POOL SHOWED ITS AGE. THE CONCRETE DECK WAS CRUMBLING AND THE AQUA-BLUE PAINT WAS PEELING. I FIGURED THEY BUILT THE POOL YEARS AGO, MAYBE AS SOME LAST DITCH EFFORT TO ATTRACT SOME OF THOSE STATION WAGONS FULL OF FAMILIES ZIPPING BY ON THE FREEWAY. THE TRAINS ACROSS THE STREET WERE HAULING THE SUMMER WHEAT HARVEST FROM A THOUSAND MIDWEST WHEAT FIELDS: HUGE GRAIN HOPPERS FULL OF WHEAT THAT SPRUNG UP LAST SPRING AND SPENT THE SUMMER UNDER BLUE SKIES AND FULL MOONS, ALIVE AND AWAKE EVERY SINGLE SECOND OF THE SUMMER THAT WAS JUST ABOUT TO END.

THIS TIME, I DON'T TAKE A SWIM,
BUT I LIE ON THE BED WITH THE
WINDOW CURTAINS OPEN, AND FALL
ASLEEP IN THE GREEN WASH OF NEON
TUBES. IN THE MORNING, I BUY A
TANK OF GAS AND A CUP OF COFFEE,
AND I START DRIVING AGAIN. JUST
LIKE YESTERDAY AND THE DAY
BEFORE YESTERDAY. DRIVING AND
SLEEPING AND DRIVING SOME MORE,
SO THAT IT'S HARD TO TELL THE
TWO THINGS APART.

TOLEDO OH.

Austin, Texas.

In Austin, summer hangs heavy and wet. When I lived there, I used to ride my bike along the river till my t-shirt was sopped with sweat and clung to my back. Tight, like a second skin over the ripple of my ribs. I rode my bike through humidity in the high percentages, past girls wearing granny glasses, and girls with blonde dreadlocks, and girls on old Schwinns riding with one pant leg rolled up. Later, I'd see those same girls at the hippy food co-op or at the punk rock record shop, and they'd still have one pant leg rolled up over the smooth rise of their calf muscle. In Austin, it was impossible to go on a simple errand without falling in love. Every time I mailed

A LETTER, OR WENT TO BUY A LOAF
OF BREAD, I'D WIND UP WITH A
BROKEN HEART.

TONIGHT, I TALK TO THAT GIRL WHO
USED TO LIVE IN AUSTIN, TOO.
THOSE WERE HER ROMANTIC YEARS,
SHE TELLS ME, WHEN SHE KISSED
MORE BOYS THAN SHE COULD COUNT.
THIS MAKES ME FEEL GRUMPY,
ENVIOUS OF ALL THOSE AUSTIN BOYS
WHO THAT GIRL HAD KISSED. I
TALK TO HER ON A PAYPHONE IN
FRONT OF A CONVENIENCE STORE
IN JUNCTION, TEXAS, EVERY TEN
MINUTES OR SO, A PICK-UP TRUCK
PULLS UP TO THE STORE, AND A
COUPLE COWBOYS GO INSIDE TO
BUY SOME BEER. THEN THEY COME
BACK OUT AND GIVE ME A LONG,
HARD STARE BEFORE SQUEALING
OUT OF THE PARKING LOT. IN
BETWEEN THE PICK-UP TRUCKS,
THERE'S SILENCE. THAT'S HOW

IT IS IN A SMALL TOWN IN SOUTH
TEXAS. A DOG BARKS. SILENCE.
A SCREEN DOOR SLAMS. SILENCE.
EVERY SOUND IS DISTINCT AND
WELL-SPACED, AS IF SOUND IN
THESE SMALL TOWNS COMES
ONLY ON A SINGLE TRACK.

COPENHAGEN, Denmark — A Lutheran minister was suspended Tuesday for saying that God doesn't exist and there is no eternal life.

Thorkild Grosboel, pastor of Taarbaek, a town of 51,000 just north of Copenhagen, said in a recent interview that "there is no heavenly God, there is no eternal life, there is no resurrection."

The statements have mystified church leaders in the Scandinavian country of 5.3 million, where about 85 percent of the population belongs to the state Evangelical Lutheran Church, yet just 5 percent attend church services regularly.

Bishop Lise-Lotte Rebel of the Helsingoer diocese, which includes Taarbaek, said Grosboel's comments "caused confusion" within the church.

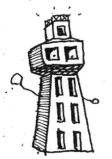

THE TOWER
GENOA, COLORADO

THE FUCKEN RAD TOUR OF THE WORLD

2.

AMATEUR
ARCHAEOLOGIST
JERRY CHUBBUCK
PULLS SOME
STUFF OUT OF A
DISPLAY CASE.

THE TOWER MUSEUM IS FULL
OF DISPLAY CASES HEAPED
WITH MYSTERY ITEMS.

"WHAT'S THIS?"
HE ASKS ME IN
A SOFT, SING-SONG
VOICE. HE HOLDS UP
SOMETHING THAT LOOKS KIND
OF LIKE A KNIFE. "IS IT A
KNIFE?" I ASK. "MAYBE IT'S
A POLACK POTATO PEELER,"
HE DEADPANS. I THINK JERRY
WANTS ME TO KEEP GUESSING,
BUT I JUST STAND THERE,
SMILING STUPIDLY. "IT'S A
MAGIC TRICK," HE FINALLY
SAYS. THEN HE SHOWS ME
HOW IT WORKS:

① ②

STAB!

JERRY ALSO SHOWS ME:

SOME WEIRD PLIERS FOR KILLING CHICKENS. OR SO HE CLAIMS.

① ②

A CIVIL WAR UNIFORM BUTTON CLAMP. THE CLAMP HOLDS THE BRASS BUTTONS STEADY SO THAT A SOLDIER COULD POLISH THEM. OR SO HE CLAIMS.

JERRY MAKES ME HOLD THIS ONE BEFORE HE TELLS ME IT'S AN INDIAN HUNTING CLUB MADE FROM AN ALASKAN WALRUS PENIS BONE.

JERRY HANDS ME A PAIR OF
BINOCULARS AND I HEAD UP
INTO THE TOWER. IT WAS
BUILT IN 1926 BY CHARLES
GREGORY ("THE P.T. BARNUM OF
COLORADO"), AND FOR YEARS, IT
WAS A POPULAR STOP ON
HIGHWAY 24. "SEE SIX
STATES!" THE HIGHWAY SIGNS
PROMISED. NOW THE TOWER IS
BYPASSED BY I-70 AND VISITORS
AREN'T EXACTLY BREAKING
DOWN THE DOORS.
UP ON THE TIPPY-TOP, WHIPPED
BY THE WIND, I FEEL LIKE I'M
IN THE CROW'S NEST OF SOME
SHIP SAILING ON THE HIGH
PLAINS INSTEAD OF THE HIGH
SEAS. I DON'T KNOW IF I'M
LOOKING AT SIX STATES, AND IT
DOESN'T EVEN MATTER.

WENDOVER, UTAH.

A HERMIT GENIUS IN UPSTATE NEW YORK CAME UP WITH SOME PLANS FOR A RAILBIKE. THE PLANS INVOLVE MODIFYING A PLAIN OLD 3-SPEED BIKE SO IT CAN RIDE ON TOP OF A RAILROAD TRACK. THE SAME GUY ALSO DESIGNED AND SELLS HIS OWN SNOWSHOE BINDINGS, AS WELL AS A SOFTWARE UTILITY PROGRAM THAT CAN "TRANSLATE HPGL AND DMPL PLOTTER FILES TO POSTSCRIPT FILES." I SPEND THE WHOLE MONTH OF OCTOBER IN WENDOVER, UTAH, LIVING IN A TRAILER OWNED BY SOME ARTISTS FROM L.A., AND CUSSING A LOT BECAUSE IT'S HARD TO BUILD A RAILBIKE. MY PLAN IS TO RIDE ON AN ABANDONED RAILROAD CALLED THE NEVADA NORTHERN. ORE TRAINS USED TO ROLL ON THESE TRACKS BETWEEN THE COPPER MINES IN RUTH, NEVADA, AND THE SMELTER IN MCGILL. BUT

NOW THE MINES ARE CLOSED AND THE SMELTER'S BEEN SCRAPPED. WHEN MY FRIEND MICHELLE COMES TO VISIT, WE LASH A SECOND BIKE TO THE FIRST ONE: MY AUNT'S OLD POWDER BLUE SCHWINN IN THE FRONT AND A NO-NAME GREEN BIKE WITH WOOD BLOCKS IN PLACE OF PEDALS IN THE REAR. THEN, ON THE VERY LAST WARM DAY OF OCTOBER, WE TAKE A RIDE, COASTING SMOOTH AND STRAIGHT OVER THE TOP OF THE SAGE BRUSH. RIDING A RAILBIKE IS LIKE FLOATING. GRAVITY HASN'T LET UP ON YOU ALTOGETHER, BUT IT HAS DECIDED TO CUT YOU SOME SLACK. THE NEXT DAY IS HALLOWEEN. WE DRIVE OUT TO SALT LAKE CITY BECAUSE MICHELLE HAS TO CATCH A PLANE. WE HAVE SOME TIME TO KILL, SO WE GO TO OLD FORT DOUGLAS WHICH IS HOSTING A

HALLOWEEN OPEN HOUSE. THE DIRECTOR OF THE MUSEUM IS A BEEFY MILITARY VET WHO NEVER CRACKS A SMILE. TONIGHT, HE'S WEARING A CIVIL WAR UNIFORM AND HE'S TELLING STORIES ABOUT CLEM, THE MUSEUM'S RESIDENT GHOST. HE TELLS US HE'S SEEN CLEM A FEW TIMES: AN ALMOST TRANSPARENT FIGURE WITH A NEATLY TRIMMED BEARD AND A 19TH CENTURY MILITARY UNIFORM. HE TELLS US CLEM'S UNIFORM IS UNUSUAL BECAUSE IT DOESN'T HAVE ANY RANK INSIGNIA. THIS DETAIL GIVES ME GOOSEBUMPS. MAYBE BECAUSE I HAVE NO IDEA WHAT IT MEANS, AND NEITHER DOES THE TOUGH OLD VET WHO MENTIONED IT. MAYBE BECAUSE IT'S NOT JUST GHOSTS THAT ARE SPOOKY, BUT THEIR LOGIC IS SPOOKY, TOO.

LATER THAT NIGHT, MICHELLE FLIES AWAY OVER SNOW CLOUDS, AND

IN THE MORNING, I DRIVE TO
COLORADO THROUGH THE SNOW THAT
FELL OUT OF THEM.

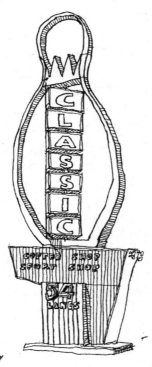

SALT LAKE CITY
STATE ST.

LUBBOCK, TX.

MY LATEST BIKE IS AN OLD SEARS
3-SPEED I BOUGHT AT A
SKETCHY USED BIKE SHOP IN
TUCSON. THERE ARE RUMORS
THE BIKES AT THAT SHOP ARE
HOT. THAT IT'S A CHOP SHOP
FOR BIKES DELIVERED IN THE
DEAD OF NIGHT. THE BEST BIKES
ARE BROKEN DOWN INTO PARTS
WHICH ARE SOLD ON THE BLACK
MARKET, WHILE OLD BEATERS
LIKE MY BIKE ARE SOLD
RIGHT OUT OF THE SHOP. I
TAKE MY LATEST BIKE BACK TO
MY HOMETOWN IN TEXAS, WHERE
THERE ARE PAVED STREETS AND
DIRT ALLEYS. THE STREETS ARE
LINED WITH HOUSES AND THE
ALLEYS ARE LINED WITH DUMP-
STERS WHERE THE PEOPLE WHO
LIVE IN THE HOUSES DUMP THEIR

TRASH. I LIKE TO RIDE MY BIKE
THROUGH THE ALLEYS. THEY'RE
A SECRET SECOND CITY, AN
ALTERNATE GRID SYSTEM OF
THIGH-HIGH TUMBLEWEEDS AND
BARKING DOGS AND TEENAGERS
SNEAKING CIGARETTES. IT'S
ALWAYS A LET-DOWN TO ROLL
BACK ONTO THE ASPHALT, BACK
ONTO THE STREETS THAT HAVE
NAMES AND NUMBERS; THE KNOWN
WORLD, ALL MAPPED AND MOWN.
A COUPLE DAYS AFTER I GET
BACK TO MY HOMETOWN, IT SNOWS.
BIG, WET SNOWFLAKES THAT YOU
CAN JUST BARELY CALL SNOW.
AFTER THE SNOW STOPS, I TAKE A
WALK AROUND THE NEIGHBORHOOD
I GREW UP IN. TWO WHOLE
DECADES AGO, I WALKED THESE
SAME SIDEWALKS LATE AT NIGHT
HOPING THAT ONE NIGHT, I'D

RUN INTO SOMEONE ELSE AS WIDE AWAKE AND RESTLESS AS ME. BUT THE ONLY PEOPLE UP THAT LATE WERE COPS AND DRUNK COWBOYS, AND IT WAS BEST NOT TO RUN INTO THOSE PEOPLE AT ALL. MAYBE SOME TECH- NOLOGY WOULD HAVE HELPED: A GLOBAL POSITIONING SATELLITE THAT TRACKS EVERY SLEEPLESS TEENAGED RAMBLER IN THE WORLD; MARKING OUR LONE- LINESS WITH COORDINATES, WITH A LATITUDE AND A LONGITUDE. MAYBE IT WOULD HAVE HELPED, A HAND-HELD COMPUTER WITH A BLACK SCREEN AND EVERY LONELY TEENAGER MARKED BY A BLINKING GREEN DOT.

MAS.

MY UNCLE'S BEEN SICK FOR A WHILE.
HE'S NOT DOING SO GREAT. WHEN
I SEE HIM TONIGHT, HE TELLS ME
HE'S BEEN HAVING STRANGE
DREAMS. HE DREAMED THAT HIS
MOM, MY GRANDMA, WAS SLEEPING
ON HIS COUCH. "WHY ARE YOU
HERE?" HE ASKED HER. "TO CHECK
UP ON YOU," SHE TELLS HIM.
"WHERE ARE YOU NOW?" HE ASKS.
"I'M NOT ALLOWED TO TELL YOU,"
SHE SAYS. "YOU WOULDN'T
RECOGNIZE ME." I ASK MY UNCLE
IF THESE DREAMS ARE SCARY.
NO, HE SAYS, THEY'RE GOOD DREAMS.
LATER ON, I RIDE MY BIKE AROUND
THE NEIGHBORHOOD. I KEEP RUNNING
INTO DEAD ENDS AND CUL-DE-SACS.
I START TO WONDER IF I'M STUCK
HERE, IN A MAZE OF SINGLE-FAMILY
HOMES WITHOUT A SINGLE FAMILY IN

46

SIGHT. JUST THE FAMILY DOGS, GONE FERAL, ROAMING THE EMPTY SIDEWALKS IN A PACK.

CRIMINAL MISCHIEF

■ 7700 block of 19th Street

A 35-year-old Lubbock man filed a complaint that his neighbor at a mobile home park vandalized his property.

The man said he had just gotten out of bed when he saw his neighbor cut his water hose, unzip his pants and urinate into his children's swimming pool. The man then stole a ball from the pool.

The victim said he does not know the suspect's name, but the neighbors have an ongoing dispute over the use of a water faucet. The victim complained that it will be a substantial inconvenience to drain and refill the pool.

PATRIOT FOUNTAIN.

MY HOMETOWN IN TEXAS JUST ERECTED
A BRAND NEW WAR MEMORIAL.
IT'S IN A PARK NEXT TO A
DRAINAGE LAKE WHERE, A FEW
MONTHS AFTER 9/11, A LOCAL
GROCERY STORE CHAIN INSTALLED
THE PATRIOT FOUNTAIN: 3 BIG JETS
OF DRAINAGE WATER THAT ARE LIT
UP AT NIGHT BY RED, WHITE, AND
BLUE SPOTLIGHTS. THE BRAND NEW
WAR MEMORIAL ISN'T LIKE THOSE
OLD CIVIL WAR MEMORIALS, OR EVEN
THE ONES FROM WORLD WAR ONE,
WHERE A MARBLE STATUE OF
WINGED VICTORY IS PERCHED ON A
PLINTH, BRANDISHING A SWORD.
THIS WAR MEMORIAL IS A BRICK
WALL SHAPED LIKE A DONUT WITH
A BITE TAKEN OUT OF IT. IN THE
MIDDLE OF THE DONUT, THERE ARE
SOME FLAGPOLES AND LITTLE
DORIC COLUMNS, AND THERE'S A

WALL OF HONOR CARVED WITH THE
NAMES OF LOCAL GUYS WHO DIED
IN EVERY WAR SINCE WWI. THE
SECTION OF THE WALL OF HONOR
SET ASIDE FOR 'OPERATION DESERT
STORM' DOESN'T LIST ANY NAMES.
IT'S THE PERFECT POST-MODERN
WAR MEMORIAL: A BLANK PIECE
OF GRANITE. A MEMORIAL TO A
NEW KIND OF WAR, FOUGHT BY
REMOTE CONTROL. WITH ALL THAT
LEFTOVER SPACE, THEY COULD AT
LEAST HAVE LISTED THE NAMES
OF SOME OF THE IRAQI CIVILIANS
WHO GOT BLOWN-UP. THE WAR
MEMORIAL IS INSCRIBED HERE
AND THERE WITH INSPIRING
QUOTES FROM ABE LINCOLN AND
GEORGE PATTON, AS WELL AS
FROM THE LOCAL GROCERY STORE
CHAIN ("UNITED SUPERMARKETS
PAYS TRIBUTE TO THE BRAVE MEN
WHO DIED ON THE FIELDS OF HONOR,
AND REMINDS SHOPPERS THAT

BRAWNY PAPER TOWELS ARE ON SALE IN AISLE SEVEN.") AND THE LOCAL PROSTHETICS SUPPLY COMPANY ("ACME PROSTHETICS COMMENDS THE BRAVE MEN WHO DIDN'T LOSE THEIR HEADS WHEN THEY LOST THEIR ARMS AND/OR LEGS ON THE FIELDS OF HONOR.") NONE OF THE MEMORIAL'S CORPORATE SPONSORS IS A GAS STATION OR AN OIL COMPANY, AND I WONDER IF THIS IS NO ACCIDENT. AFTER A FEW VISITS, THE MEMORIAL STARTS TO FREAK ME OUT. MAYBE BECAUSE I SUSPECT IT WASN'T BUILT SO MUCH TO MEMORIALIZE PEOPLE WHO DIED IN PAST WARS AS TO SUPPORT THE CURRENT ADMINI-STRATION AND ITS CURRENT WAR. OR MAYBE BECAUSE IT LOOKS LIKE SOMETHING DESIGNED BY A TEAM OF STRIP MALL REAL ESTATE

DEVELOPERS IN LEAGUE WITH A TEAM OF FUNERAL PARLOR DIRECTORS. THE MONUMENT IS CONSTRUCTED OF TAN-COLORED BRICKS, AND IT'S LIT UP BY THOUGHTFULLY DESIGNED LIGHTING. IT'S TASTEFUL, IN A WAY THAT REDUCES ALL THE GRISLY HORROR OF WAR TO SOMETHING SURE NOT TO OFFEND ANYBODY. IT'S A MEMORIAL THAT'S SUITABLE FOR GRADE SCHOOL FIELD TRIPS. IT'S A READER'S DIGEST VERSION OF LOSS AND GRIEF AND DREAD. I CONSIDER MAKING A SPRAYPAINT STENCIL THAT SAYS "PLEASE BLOW ME UP" AND TAGGING THE MEMORIAL WITH IT. BUT THEN I FIGURE A) I'D GET IN REALLY BIG TROUBLE, AND B) NO ONE WOULD.

HOLBROOK, ARIZONA

I PULL OFF INTERSTATE 40 AT THE
HOPI TRAVEL PLAZA, AN ENORMOUS
STEEL SHED WITH A BURGER
KING INSIDE. THERE'S ALSO A
GAME ROOM, AND A SOUVENIR
SHOP THAT SELLS DREAM CATCHERS
AND NAVAJO RUGS AND BUMPER
STICKERS THAT SAY STUFF LIKE
"HOW'S MY DRIVING? DIAL
1-800-EAT-SHIT." ON THE WAY
TO THE BATHROOM, I PASS A
STAIRWAY AND A SIGN THAT SAYS
"TRUCKER CHAPEL." I'M CURIOUS
TO SEE A TRUCKER CHAPEL, SO I
GO UPSTAIRS. I HAVE AN IDEA
IT'LL BE LIKE THE SISTINE
CHAPEL, EXCEPT THE FRESCOES
PAINTED ON THE CEILING WILL
SHOW ADAM AND EVE AS A

TRUCKER COUPLE IN THE FRONT
SEAT OF A BIG RIG, AND GOD
WILL BE THE DISPATCHER, CALLING
THEM UP ON SOME HEAVENLY C.B.
AT THE TOP OF THE STAIRS,
THERE'S ANOTHER SIGN:
"TRUCKER SHOWERS AND JACUZZI,"
WITH AN ARROW POINTING TO THE
LEFT, "TRUCKER CHAPEL," WITH
AN ARROW POINTING TO THE
RIGHT. THIS SIGN SEEMS LIKE A
TEST. A MOMENT OF TRUCKER
TRUTH. DO YOU CHOOSE THE PATH
OF RIGHTEOUSNESS, OR DO YOU
CHOOSE THE JACUZZI?
AN OLDER GUY IS LOITERING IN
FRONT OF THE DOOR TO THE
CHAPEL. AT FIRST, I FIGURE HE'S
A TRUCKER WHO'S NOT SURE
HE WANTS TO GO INSIDE. BUT

THEN HE HOLDS OUT HIS HAND.
"HELLO," HE SAYS, "I'M DAVE."
"HI," I SAY, "IS IT OKAY IF I
TAKE A PEEK INSIDE?" DAVE OPENS
THE DOOR. "COME ON IN." DAVE
IS WEARING A STARCHED BLUE
T-SHIRT. IT'S GOT A DRAWING
OF AN 18-WHEELER PARKED IN
FRONT OF A LITTLE CHAPEL.
THE CHAPEL HAS A COUPLE STAINED
GLASS WINDOWS AND A STEEPLE
WITH A CROSS ON TOP. IT'S NOT
A PICTURE OF THE ACTUAL
TRUCKER CHAPEL, BUT THE IDEA
OF THE TRUCKER CHAPEL, WHICH
HAS SOMETHING TO DO WITH
OLD TIME RELIGION, AND SMALL
TOWNS, AND ALL-AMERICAN
VALUES. "TRUCK STOP MINISTRIES,"
THE SHIRT SAYS. DAVE'S PROBABLY

A PERFECTLY NICE GUY, BUT HE GIVES ME THIS LOOK; THE SAME LOOK, I IMAGINE, THAT HE GIVES HIS T-BONE JUST BEFORE HE DIGS IN. "SORRY, I'M ACTUALLY IN KIND OF A RUSH," I STUTTER, BACKING UP TOWARD THE STAIRS. "BUT THANKS ANYWAY." "DO YOU HAVE A BIBLE?" DAVE CALLS AFTER ME. "YES. I MEAN, NO. I MEAN, NO THANKS." THEN I HURRY DOWN THE STAIRS, PRETTY SURE I KNOW WHAT DAVE'S THINKING. THAT THESE STAIRS DON'T JUST LEAD TO THE BURGER KING ON THE FIRST FLOOR, BUT KEEP GOING. DOWN, DOWN, DOWN.

ALBUQUERQUE
CENTRAL AVE. (RT. 66)

Border #1

I spend the day bumping through the desert with some border activists. The eastern California desert is hard baked clay, and the only shelter is the shadows cast by some spiny little shrubs. The activists, mostly from L.A., maintain a network of water stations out in the desert: blue barrels full of gallon jugs of water, and marked by a blue flag that whips and snaps on top of a tall metal pole. A lot of migrants from Mexico walk across the open desert. The activists think the water

STATIONS HELP, BUT EVEN SO, NOT EVERYONE MAKES IT ACROSS THE DESERT ALIVE. JOHN, THE GUY WHO STARTED THE WATER PROJECT, WAS ONCE FEATURED IN POPULAR MECHANICS FOR DESIGNING THE WORLD'S LARGEST GUN. NOW HE SPLITS HIS TIME BETWEEN DESIGNING TOYS AND LEAVING BOTTLES OF WATER IN THE CALIFORNIA DESERT.

AFTER DARK, WE HEAD BACK TO THE MOTEL IN OCOTILLO. THERE ISN'T MUCH TO OCOTILLO: A GAS STATION, A BAR, AND THE OCOTILLO TRAILER MOTEL. A MIDDLE-AGED LADY NAMED MITZY RUNS THE PLACE. IT ISN'T A REGULAR MOTEL, BUT A COLLECTION OF OLD TRAVEL

TRAILERS AND MOBILE HOMES. IT'D MAKE A GOOD HIDE-OUT, THAT MOTEL. MITZY GRILLS UP SOME CARNE ASADA BY THE SWIMMING POOL. A COUPLE LOCAL GUYS SIT AT A TABLE DRINKING BEER. THERE'S A KARAOKE MACHINE IN THE CORNER. IT'S UNPLUGGED. THAT NIGHT, I STAY IN ROOM 1. MITZY TELLS ME IT'S THE ROOM WHERE THE WRESTLER EL GORDO ONCE STAYED. ROOM 1 HAS A SAGGING EL GORDO-SIZED BED AND A FEW EL GORDO-SIZED COCKROACHES. I LIE DOWN ON THE BED AND FEEL SAFE AND SECRET. THE WAY YOU FEEL WHEN YOU'VE GOTTEN YOURSELF LOST IN THE WORLD. THE WAY YOU FEEL WHEN NO ONE CAN FIND YOU.

Border #2

I TAG ALONG WITH HECTOR, A
REALLY NICE KID FROM L.A.
WHO'S SPENDING HIS SUMMER IN
ARIVACA, ARIZONA, DOWN ALONG
THE BORDER. HE'S VOLUNTEERING
WITH A GROUP CALLED THE
SAMARITANS, WHO DRIVE AROUND
THE DESERT SOUTH OF TUCSON
LOOKING FOR MIGRANTS IN
TROUBLE. WHEN YOU'RE HIKING
ACROSS THE SONORAN DESERT
IN THE MIDDLE OF SUMMER, IT'S
NOT HARD TO GET INTO TROUBLE.
WE DRIVE AROUND ALL MORNING,
STOPPING AT A FEW DRY WASHES.
WE FIND LOTS OF EMPTY WATER
BOTTLES BUT NO PEOPLE. JUST
BEFORE WE HEAD BACK, HECTOR

TRIES ONE LAST PLACE, A CAMP
HE KNOWS ABOUT HIDDEN IN
THE SCRUB. AS WE HIKE IN, A
COUPLE GUYS APPROACH US.
LATER, HECTOR TELLS ME HE
DIDN'T LIKE THE LOOKS OF THESE
GUYS. THEY KEPT EXCHANGING
GLANCES, AND ONE OF THEM
KEPT HIS HAND IN HIS POCKET.
HECTOR TELLS ME THEY LOOKED
LIKE THE KIND OF GUYS IN HIS
NEIGHBORHOOD IN L.A. WHO YOU'D
WANT TO AVOID. HECTOR TALKS
TO THE GUYS. TELLS THEM WE'VE
GOT WATER. SUDDENLY, A
COUPLE MORE PEOPLE COME OUT
OF THE BRUSH, A GUY AND A
GIRL IN THEIR 20'S WHO SPEAK
ENGLISH AND DON'T SEEM TOO
HAPPY TO SEE US. BASICALLY

THEY TELL US NO THANKS FOR THE WATER AND COULD WE PLEASE GET LOST? BACK IN THE CAR, HECTOR TELLS ME THE GUY AND THE GIRL WERE PROBABLY COYOTES — SMUGGLERS LEADING A GROUP OF MIGRANTS THROUGH THE DESERT. HECTOR TELLS ME SOME COYOTES ARE OKAY, BUT SOME ARE CREEPY. GANGSTERS OUT FOR A QUICK BUCK WHO DON'T THINK TWICE ABOUT DITCHING THE PEOPLE THEY'RE GUIDING IF THEY RUN INTO TROUBLE. ALL THIS SKETCHINESS MAKES HECTOR MAD. IT SHOULDN'T BE LIKE THIS. PEOPLE SHOULDN'T HAVE TO RISK THEIR LIVES JUST TO GET A JOB IN THE U.S. THAT NOBODY ELSE WANTS.

BACK IN TUCSON, SARAH'S SWAMP
COOLER STOPS WORKING.
EVAPORATIVE COOLERS ONLY WORK
WHEN THE HUMIDITY IS LOW,
THE WAY IT USUALLY IS IN TUCSON.
BUT NOW THE HUMIDITY IS
RISING, AND FOR THE LAST FEW
AFTERNOONS, THE SKY HAS BEEN
FILLING UP WITH PUFFY WHITE
CLOUDS. OUT ON THE SIDEWALK,
THE PEOPLE YOU PASS DON'T
SAY "HELLO" ANYMORE, BUT
"IT'S COMING," OR "ANY DAY NOW,"
AND YOU KNOW EXACTLY WHAT
THEY'RE TALKING ABOUT. THEY'RE
TALKING ABOUT THE RAIN. ONE
AFTERNOON, WHILE I'M SITTING ON
SARAH'S PORCH, THE CLOUDS THAT
ROLL IN LOOK DARKER AND
SCARIER THAN USUAL. THE

CICADAS IN THE PALO VERDE
TREES START TO BUZZ AT FULL
VOLUME, LIKE THE STRING
SECTION IN A HITCHCOCK FILM:
EE! EE! EE! THEN, WITHOUT
WARNING, THE WIND HITS. IT
KNOCKS OVER ALL THE PLASTIC
OUTDOOR CHAIRS AND SETS ALL
THE WIND CHIMES CHIMING —
NO SMALL THING IN TUCSON,
A MIGHTY METROPOLIS OF
PLASTIC OUTDOOR CHAIRS AND
WIND CHIMES. A LIGHTNING
BOLT FLASHES. THEN ANOTHER.
AS THE FIRST FAT DROPS OF RAIN
SMACK INTO THE GROUND, THE
YARD CATS, A HALF-DOZEN OF
THEM, TAKE SHELTER WITH
ME ON THE PORCH. A FEW
SECONDS LATER, IT'S POURING,

AND I RUN INTO THE YARD AND
STAND THERE TILL I'M SOPPING
WET. JUST TO BE SURE,
100-PERCENT POSITIVE, THAT
THE MONSOON RAINS HAVE
FINALLY COME.

TUCSON SECTOR DEATHS

17 heat exposure
1 train accident
5 vehicle accidents
2 homicides
26 unknown
51 total

Source: U.S. Border Patrol

SAN DIEGO

IN SAN DIEGO, PEOPLE SLEEP IN
THEIR CONDOS AND LIVE IN THEIR
CARS AND ALL YOUR FRIENDS
ARE CELL PHONE NUMBERS.
THE SIDEWALKS ARE SIBERIA.
THEY'RE WHERE THE EXILES ARE
EXILED TO: CRAZY PEOPLE AND
PEOPLE WITHOUT CARS AND
PEOPLE WHO'VE HAD THEIR
DRIVER'S LICENSE REVOKED. WHEN
YOU'RE EXILED TO THE SIDEWALK,
YOU WALK NEXT TO ALL THE
CARS PARKED ALONG THE CURB.
THAT'S WHEN YOU NOTICE THAT
EVERY CAR'S GOT A NOTE TUCKED
UNDER ITS WINDSHIELD WIPER
BLADE. IN SAN DIEGO, STRANGERS
DON'T TALK TO EACH OTHER IN

PERSON, BUT LEAVE NOTES UNDER EACH OTHER'S WIPER BLADES. LOTS OF NOTES, COMPLAINING ABOUT STOLEN PARKING SPACES OR CONFESSING TO DENTED FENDERS. HATE NOTES AND LOVE NOTES AND ADVERTISING FLYERS FOR CHINESE TAKE-OUT. SOME PEOPLE READ THE NOTES, AND SOME PEOPLE DON'T BOTHER. INSTEAD, THEY DRIVE ONTO THE FREEWAY AND LET THE WIND TAKE CARE OF THE REST.

CARLSBAD, CALIFORNIA.

I PULL OFF I-5 AT MIDNIGHT AND
PARK AT A DENNY'S IN CARLSBAD.
I SLEEP AN HOUR AT A TIME.
EVERY HOUR, SOMETHING WAKES
ME UP — A CAR FULL OF DRUNK
FRAT BOYS, OR A CAR FULL OF
DRUNK SURFERS, OR A CAR FULL
OF DRUNK HIGH SCHOOL KIDS. THEN
I MOVE MY CAR TO A DIFFERENT
PARKING SPACE, HOPING TO FIND
JUST THE RIGHT SPACE, THE ONE
WHERE I'LL SLEEP CLEAR THROUGH
THE NIGHT. JUST BEFORE THE SUN COMES
UP, I STRAIGHTEN MY SHIRT AND
PUSH DOWN MY HAIR. THEN I GO
INSIDE THE DENNY'S FOR A CUP
OF COFFEE AND A COUPLE SLICES
OF WHEAT TOAST. THE WAITRESS IS
A SURFER GIRL ON THE LAST HALF-
HOUR OF AN ALL-NIGHT SHIFT.
SHE ASKS ME IF I'M THE GUY WHO

DELIVERS THE NEWSPAPERS TO THE
BOXES OUT FRONT. I ALMOST TELL
HER NO, I'M THE GUY WHO SLEEPS
IN THE PARKING LOT ALL NIGHT.
OUTSIDE, THE SKY IS JUST BEGINNING
TO BRIGHTEN. AT SOME POINT, IT'S
HARD TO SAY EXACTLY WHEN,
SATURDAY NIGHT STOPS AND SUNDAY
MORNING BEGINS. INSIDE, THE
DENNY'S IS STARTING TO SHIFT, TOO.
PEOPLE WHO'VE BEEN OUT ALL NIGHT
FINISH THEIR LAST CUPS OF COFFEE,
AND PEOPLE WHO'VE JUST GOTTEN
UP ASK FOR A MENU. A COUPLE OF
OLD EARLY-BIRDS IN THE CORNER
ARE TRYING HARD TO IGNORE THE
TWO DRUNK CLUB KIDS AT THE NEXT
TABLE WHO KEEP HASSLING THE
WAITRESS FOR MORE COFFEE AND
TABASCO SAUCE. THE SURFER
WAITRESS TAKES IT ALL IN STRIDE,
HAPPY, I GUESS, TO HAVE SURVIVED
THE 3-AM RUSH, AND HAPPY FOR

THIS SLOW SPELL JUST BEFORE SHE GETS OFF WORK. AT 5:30, THE WAITRESS SAYS ADIOS TO THE SHORT-ORDER COOKS. BUT THEN SHE DOESN'T LEAVE. SHE BUSSES A FEW MORE TABLES AND CASHES OUT THE DRUNK KIDS. LIKE SHE'S RELUCTANT TO GO, TO JUST SLIP OUT THE DOOR WITHOUT CEREMONY AFTER PUTTING IN SO MANY HARD HOURS AT THIS PLACE. SHE TAKES ONE LAST LOOK AROUND THE DINING ROOM. "OKAY, I'M REALLY GOING TO LEAVE NOW." THEN SHE DOES. THE MORNING GUY AT THE REGISTER DOESN'T EVEN BOTHER TO LOOK UP. I WATCH THE SURFER WAITRESS WALK ACROSS THE EMPTY PARKING LOT TO HER CAR. SHE TAKES OFF HER GREEN DENNY'S APRON AND TOSSES IT IN THE BACK SEAT. AND I WISH I COULD PRESS SOME SECRET BUTTON, HIDDEN BEHIND

THE RACK OF JAM PACKETS ON MY
TABLE, OR UNDER THE LITTLE
SYRUP DISPENSERS, THREE OF THEM,
EACH ONE WITH A DIFFERENT
FLAVOR OF SYRUP. A SECRET
BUTTON THAT WOULD FIRE OFF A
SKYROCKET OR TWO FOR THAT
WAITRESS JUST OFF THE GRAVE-
YARD SHIFT.

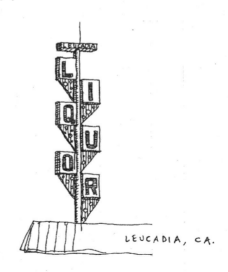

LEUCADIA, CA.

LOS ANGELES.

THOM AND I GET BREAKFAST AT A DINER IN SILVER LAKE CALLED THE BRITE SPOT. IT'S A GREASY SPOON, BUT YOU CAN STILL ORDER STUFF LIKE EGGS BENEDICT WITH TOFU INSTEAD OF EGGS. THOM SAYS THAT EVERY WORKING CLASS BAR AND DINER IN THIS PART OF THE CITY HAS BEEN TAKEN OVER BY HIPSTER KIDS. HE REFERS TO THIS AS "THE EXTINCTION OF WORKING CLASS LEISURE SPACE."

THE NEXT MORNING, MY FRIEND JOHN TAKES ME TO A NO-FRILLS RESTAURANT IN LONG BEACH WHERE BREAKFAST COSTS A BUCK. THE OTHER CUSTOMERS ARE MOSTLY OLDER GUYS WHO SEEM DOWN ON THEIR LUCK. MOST OF THEM ARE SITTING ALONE. THE WAITRESS IS YOUNG AND SHE'S ACTING AWFULLY

FORMAL. "HOW ARE WE DOING?"
SHE ASKS, AND "WOULD YOU
GENTLEMEN CARE FOR A REFILL?"
HER POLITENESS MAKES ME EDGY.
I WHISPER TO JOHN THAT I
THINK THIS PLACE IS RUN BY A
CULT. MAYBE EVEN THE
SCIENTOLOGISTS. HE TELLS ME THAT
WHEN BREAKFAST COSTS A BUCK,
I SHOULDN'T ASK TOO MANY
QUESTIONS.

OLD CANOGA PARK LIBRARY
ABANDONED.
L.A.

Buttonwillow, CA.

I want to ask the kid at the front desk if it's a good job or a bad job, working at the motel 6 in Buttonwillow, CA. I want to ask him if he's glad to be working just off the freeway that runs from the border of Mexico to the border of Canada, so that if he ever has a bad night, he can just hop on the highway and, pretty soon, he'll be a thousand miles away. Or maybe it's a crappy job, and all the people who check in from all those faraway freeway cities just remind the kid that he's stuck here working another grave-yard shift. Buttonwillow is in the central valley, and it's not so much a town as

A COLLECTION OF MOTELS AND FAST
FOOD JOINTS. IF YOU'VE EVER
DREAMED ABOUT CALIFORNIA,
THIS PROBABLY ISN'T THE PLACE
YOU WERE DREAMING ABOUT.

I FELT THE SAME WAY ABOUT
HOLLYWOOD, THE FIRST TIME I
VISITED. I GUESS I EXPECTED
SWIMMING POOLS AND MOVIE STARS,
SO IT WAS A SURPRISE TO FIND
RUNAWAYS AND BAD HEROIN. A
SURPRISE TO FIND THE KIND OF PLACE
WHERE YOU RENT A CHEAP ROOM
AND WONDER HOW YOUR LIFE
STALLED HERE, A FEW MILES
SHORT OF THE SEA. HOLLYWOOD
IS A PLACE TO GET MUGGED; AND
THE MOJAVE DESERT IS FULL OF
METH LABS; AND THE GOLDEN
GATE BRIDGE STRADDLES A FAULT
LINE; AND HIPPY KIDS ARMED
WITH MACHINE GUNS HARVEST

POT UP IN HUMBOLDT COUNTY; AND
BUTTONWILLOW, CA. IS HAZED
OVER BY PESTICIDES THAT SMELL
SWEET LIKE CUT FLOWERS.
NONE OF WHICH IS THE CALIFORNIA
YOU DREAM ABOUT, AT LEAST NOT
UNTIL YOU SPEND SOME TIME IN
THE STATE. THEN, PRETTY SOON,
THIS IS THE CALIFORNIA YOUR
DREAMS ARE FULL OF.

RATON, NM

EUREKA, CALIFORNIA.

I'M TOO STUPID TO KNOW THAT IT'S
STUPID TO CROSS THE COAST
RANGE AT MIDNIGHT. AT TIMES,
THE FOG IS SO THICK THAT I
HAVE TO SLOW TO A CRAWL,
PRAYING THAT SOME SPEED FREAK
TRUCKER DOESN'T PLOW INTO ME
FROM BEHIND. MY HEADLIGHTS
ARE USELESS. THEY JUST BOUNCE
BACK AT ME. FROM SOMEWHERE
ELSE, IT PROBABLY LOOKS PRETTY.
LIKE EVERY CAR IS A LITTLE
LUMINESCENT CLOUD FLOATING
SLOWLY DOWN THE FACE OF THE
MOUNTAINS. BUT INSIDE MY CAR,
IT'S NOT PRETTY AT ALL. AT
SOME POINT, THE FOG BEGINS TO
SMELL LIKE THE SEA, AND NEXT
THING I KNOW, I'M DRIVING INTO
EUREKA. I STOP AT A FLYING-S

GAS STATION FOR A TANK OF GAS
AND A BOTTLE OF WATER. WHEN
I PULL OUT MY WALLET TO PAY,
I NOTICE MY HANDS ARE
SHAKING. I STAND IN LINE
BEHIND A SKINNY GUY
WEARING A FISHERMAN'S HAT.
HE WHISPERS SOMETHING TO THE
GIRL AT THE REGISTER. SHE
SHAKES HER HEAD. WHEN IT'S
MY TURN AT THE REGISTER, SHE
TELLS ME THE GUY JUST OFFERED
HER SOME WEED FOR A CORN
DOG. SHE SNORTS. "LIKE I DON'T
ALREADY GOT ENOUGH WEED,"
SHE SAYS.

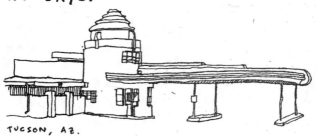

TUCSON, AZ.

LAS VEGAS, NM.

THE TRAIN IS ALREADY AN HOUR LATE.
NO ONE'S SURPRISED. "YOU'RE DOING
PRETTY GOOD IF IT'S LESS THAN 5
HOURS LATE," A GUY AT THE
CONVENIENCE STORE TELLS ME.
THE ONLY OTHER PERSON WAITING
FOR THE TRAIN IS A NATIVE
AMERICAN GUY WITH BRAIDED PIG
TAILS THAT GO ALL THE WAY DOWN
TO HIS HIPS. NEXT DOOR TO THE
TRAIN STATION IS AN ABANDONED
RAILROAD HOTEL. AN OLD HARVEY
HOUSE, WITH RED SPANISH TILES
ON THE ROOF AND CURVY MISSION
REVIVAL GABLES. IN THE LATE
1800's, A GUY NAMED FRED HARVEY
RAN A WHOLE CHAIN OF THE
HOTELS ALONG THE RAILROADS OF
THE U.S. HARVEY WAS FAMOUS FOR
HIS HIGH STANDARDS. HE WAS ALSO
FAMOUS FOR STAFFING HIS REST-
AURANTS WITH YOUNG WOMEN —

HARVEY GIRLS — WHO PROBABLY
HAD TO FEND OFF COUNTLESS PATHETIC
TRAIN PASSENGER CRUSHES.

THE TRAIN IS TWO HOURS LATE
WHEN A YOUNG GUY WALKS INTO
THE STATION. HE LOOKS CONFUSED.
"WHERE DO YOU BUY A TICKET?"
HE ASKS ME IN A THICK ACCENT.
IT TURNS OUT HE'S FROM NEPAL.
HE TELLS ME HE'S FROM THE FLAT
PART. 12% OF NEPAL IS FLAT, AND
THE REST IS THE HIMALAYAS. I
TELL THE KID HE CAN'T BUY A
TRAIN TICKET HERE. HE STARES
AT ME. "ISN'T THIS THE TRAIN
STATION?" I TELL HIM IT IS.
"BUT YOU CAN'T BUY A TRAIN
TICKET HERE?" I SHAKE MY
HEAD. THEN WE BOTH START
LAUGHING. I EXPLAIN THAT YOU
CAN ONLY BUY TICKETS ONLINE,
OR DOWN IN ALBUQUERQUE. I
EXPLAIN THAT MOST PEOPLE IN
THE U.S. DON'T RIDE THE TRAIN,

WHICH GOES DOUBLE FOR LAS VEGAS, NEW MEXICO.

THE KID FROM NEPAL TELLS ME HOW HE WOUND UP IN THIS TOWN. HE'D NEVER BEEN TO THE U.S. BEFORE, SO WHEN HE WAS APPLYING TO COLLEGES, HE DECIDED TO STICK TO CITIES HE'D AT LEAST HEARD OF. LAS VEGAS SEEMED LIKE A GOOD CHOICE. A FAMOUS CENTER OF ENTERTAINMENT. A RESORT TOWN. BUT THEN HE GOT TO LAS VEGAS, AND IT WASN'T WHAT HE'D EXPECTED. IT WASN'T BIG OR EXCITING. IN FACT, IT WAS KIND OF RUN-DOWN AND SLEEPY, AND WHERE WERE ALL THE CASINOS? SOMEONE AT HIS COLLEGE FINALLY SET HIM STRAIGHT. HE'D CHOSEN THE WRONG LAS VEGAS.

THE TRAIN FINALLY ROLLS IN, THREE HOURS LATE. THE KID FROM THE 12% OF NEPAL THAT'S FLAT SHAKES MY HAND GOODBYE. THEN I CLIMB ABOARD THE TRAIN AND SIT DOWN, AND THE CONDUCTOR WRITES "CHI" ON A LITTLE SLIP OF PAPER AND STICKS IT ABOVE MY SEAT. CHICAGO. "ARE YOU READY, GLEN?" A VOICE ASKS OVER THE CONDUCTOR'S WALKIE-TALKIE. "READY," GLEN SAYS. "LET'S HIGHBALL," WHICH IN TRAIN TALK MEANS "LET 'ER RIP." IT'S A ROMANTIC WORD TO USE, ALL FRAGRANT WITH COAL SMOKE AND OLD STOGIES AND HOBO STEW BOILED UP IN A TIN CAN. SO WHAT IF IT'S JUST A DORKY OLD AMTRAK TRAIN THAT'S RUNNING THREE HOURS LATE? WE'RE STILL ROLLING ON THE HIGHLINE TO CHICAGO, AND WE'RE

STILL GOING TO BUST THROUGH
EVERY SLEEPY LITTLE FARM
TOWN FOR THE NEXT THOUSAND
MILES.

AMTRAK STATION
LA JUNTA, CO.

HICAGO

I VISIT S.C. AT THE BAR WHERE SHE WORKS, JUST BEFORE CLOSING TIME. WHILE SHE CASHES OUT, I CHAT WITH THE MANAGER, A TOUGH-AS-NAILS WOMAN FROM FINLAND WHO RACES MOTORCYCLES FOR FUN. SHE TELLS ME THAT IN CHICAGO, SOME BARS CLOSE AT 2AM AND SOME CLOSE AT 4. I ASK HER WHAT THE DIFFERENCE IS, AND THE GUY SWEEPING THE FLOOR BUTTS IN: "A 2AM BAR IS WHERE YOU TAKE YOUR GIRLFRIEND. A 4AM BAR IS WHERE YOU GO TO GET PUSSY." THE MANAGER ROLLS HER EYES. "DORK," SHE SAYS.

S.C. AND I WALK DOWN DAMEN.
IT'S A QUARTER TO 3 AND THE
STREET IS EMPTY. NO CARS.
JUST THE FLAT ORANGE WASH
OF THE STREETLIGHTS THAT
WIPE OUT THE SHADOWS AND
THE STARS, AND MAKE ME FEEL
LIKE WE'RE NOT ON THE STREET,
BUT IN SOME VAST, WELL-LIT
WAREHOUSE THAT'S GOT A
WHOLE CITY STORED INSIDE IT.
I MOVED AWAY FROM CHICAGO
A FEW YEARS BACK, AND I TELL
S.C. THAT VISITING THE PLACE
NOW FEELS LIKE RUNNING INTO
AN OLD GIRLFRIEND OR BOYFRIEND.
EVERYTHING IS POLITE BUT
NOTHING IS THE SAME.
WE TURN ONTO CHICAGO AVE. AND
WALK PAST THE "DOLLAR MARKET"

WHERE I BOUGHT A COUPLE BLANK
VIDEO TAPES THE OTHER DAY
FOR $1.60 A PIECE. I TELL S.C.
THAT THE PLACE SHOULD CHANGE
ITS NAME TO THE "DOLLAR-SIXTY
MARKET," BUT S.C. ARGUES THAT
I'M CONFUSING THE "DOLLAR MARKET"
WITH THE "EVERYTHING UNDER A
DOLLAR STORE." MAYBE SHE'S
RIGHT. OR MAYBE THE DOLLAR
MARKET'S NAME IS VESTIGIAL,
DATING FROM A TIME WHEN EVERY-
THING IN THE STORE WAS JUST
A BUCK. SORT OF LIKE 7-11
(WHEN THOSE WERE ITS HOURS)
OR MOTEL 6 (WHEN THAT'S HOW
MUCH A ROOM COST). MAYBE THE
WHOLE WORLD IS MISNAMED, OR
NAMED FOR AN EARLIER, OBSOLETE
VERSION OF ITSELF. THE WORLD
THAT'S NAMED IN ALL THESE

STORE SIGNS IS A LOST WORLD,
AND THE NEW WORLD, THE
WORLD WE'VE GOT NOW, IS STILL
WAITING FOR A NAME.

I SLEEP ON THE COUCH IN MY OLD
APARTMENT, AND WHEN I WAKE
UP, I CAN'T REMEMBER WHERE
I AM. ON A TRAIN OR A BUS,
IT'S SUPPOSED TO BE LIKE THAT.
YOU FALL ASLEEP IN ONE CITY
AND WAKE UP IN ANOTHER. BUT
WHEN YOU SLEEP ON A COUCH, YOU
EXPECT TO WAKE UP IN THE SAME
CITY YOU FELL ASLEEP IN, AND
YOU SHOULDN'T HAVE TO LOOK
OUT THE WINDOW TO FIGURE OUT
WHAT CITY THAT IS. I GET UP
AND LOOK OUT THE WINDOW.
"OH YEAH," I SAY TO MYSELF,
"CHICAGO."

CHICAGO.

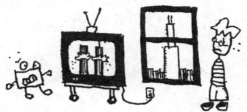

THE DAY THE TWIN TOWERS
GOT HIT, I REMEMBER
LOOKING OUT MY WINDOW
AT THE SEARS TOWER AND
WONDERING IF IT'D BE NEXT.

A COUPLE DAYS LATER,
THE CITY ERECTED
CONCRETE BARRICADES
AROUND THE BUILDING.
AS IF THAT'D HELP.
THEY PAINTED THE
BARRICADES RED,
WHITE, AND BLUE,
AND EVEN THREW IN
SOME STARS.

WHEN I WAS A KID, I USED TO DREAM ABOUT LIVING IN A SKY-SCRAPER. A HUNDRED STORIES UP, LIVING AMONG THE HELICOPTERS AND THE CLOUDS.

BUT ALL THE SUDDEN, MY 2-STORY APARTMENT BUILDING ON WALNUT STREET SEEMED PLENTY HIGH ENOUGH.

TOLEDO

THE TRAIN IS LATE, SO I TAKE A
WALK. NOT FAR FROM THE
STATION IS AN OLD WAREHOUSE.
"GREAT LAKES COLD STORAGE"
IS PAINTED ON THE SIDE IN
TWO-STORY TALL LETTERS. I
DECIDE THIS IS WHERE THEY'RE
KEPT.   1 AM'S LIKE THIS ONE.
HOURS THAT ARE USEFUL FOR
JUST 60 MINUTES AND THEN
BECOME OBSOLETE. THEY'RE
CRATED UP AND STACKED IN
COLD STORAGE WAREHOUSES IN
CITIES THAT HAVE SEEN BETTER
DAYS.

WHEN THE TRAIN FINALLY SHOWS
UP, IT'S OVERBOOKED, THANKS
TO A GROUP OF 40 JUNIOR

MARINES WHO GET ON BOARD AHEAD
OF ME ; A BUNCH OF CREW CUT
KIDS LED BY A GUY WHO LOOKS
LIKE A KINDLY OLD MARINE,
BUT TURNS OUT TO BE A LOUD-
MOUTH PRICK, PROVING THAT OLD
SOLDIERS NEVER DIE, THEY JUST
WIND UP CHAPERONING NAZI
YOUTH ACROSS COUNTRY ON
AMTRAK. THERE AREN'T ANY
SEATS, SO I SIT AT A TABLE IN
THE LOUNGE CAR AND TRY TO
SLEEP, SLUMPED OVER LIKE A
DRUNK GUY AT AN ALL NIGHT DINER.
ONLY THIS DINER IS ON WHEELS.
A HOBO DINER, RIDING THE RAILS
ACROSS OHIO IN THE MIDDLE OF
THE NIGHT.

FOURTEEN HOURS LATER, I'M IN
NEW YORK AND I'M FEELING

KIND OF DAZED. YESTERDAY, I WAS
IN A CITY FULL OF SHUTTERED
    FACTORIES, AND TODAY I'M
IN A CITY WHERE EVEN THE
TRAFFIC REPORTS ON THE RADIO
ARE SELECTIVE, REPORTING ONLY
THE A-LIST ACCIDENTS. THE
ONES THAT HAVE GOTTEN SOME
BUZZ. A CITY WHERE YOU HAVE
TO HAVE CONNECTIONS TO GET
INTO A TECHNO CLUB, OR FIND
AN APARTMENT, OR EVEN GET
YOUR CAR ACCIDENT MENTIONED
BY THE TRAFFIC REPORTER ON
THE RADIO.

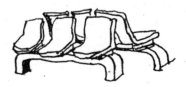

LAKESHORE LIMITED.

ON THE TRAIN, YOU SLEEP IN FITS.
NOT THE SMOOTH SLEEP OF A
TRANS-ATLANTIC RED EYE SOARING
THROUGH STARRY SKIES, BUT A
SLEEP THAT'S INTERRUPTED BY
EVERY STATION STOP. EVERY
TIME YOU OPEN YOUR EYES, THERE'S
ANOTHER TRAIN STATION OUTSIDE
THE WINDOW MARKED WITH THE
NAME OF ANOTHER CITY. IT'S
AS IF THE DREAM YOU'RE DREAMING
WHILE YOU SLEEP ON THE TRAIN
HAS ITS OWN SCHEDULED STOPS
THAT PRECISELY CORRESPOND WITH
THE STOPS THE TRAIN MAKES.
BUT NOW I'M AWAKE, THANKS TO
THE GUY WHO'S SNORING IN THE SEAT
BEHIND ME. NOT JUST SNORING,
BUT MAKING AN INCREDIBLY LOUD
WHEEZING NOISE THAT STARTS DEEP
IN HIS CHEST AND RATTLES
THROUGH HIS SINUSES. IN OLD WEST

STORIES, THE EXCESSIVE CRUELTY OF A PARTICULAR OUTLAW IS OFTEN UNDERSCORED BY REVEALING THAT "HE ONCE SHOT A MAN DEAD JUST FOR SNORING." AND WHILE I DON'T EXACTLY CONDONE MURDERING PEOPLE WHO SNORE, I CAN AT LEAST SYMPATHIZE WITH THE IMPULSE. I MEAN, AFTER A LONG DAY OF ROBBING BANKS AND BEING CHASED BY LAWMEN, THE LAST THING YOU NEED IS SOME COWBOY WITH A DEVIATED SEPTUM RUINING YOUR SLEEP.

HOURS LATER, THE LAKESHORE LIMITED PULLS INTO PENN STATION IN NEW YORK. PENN STATION USED TO BE ONE OF THE WORLD'S GREAT TRAIN STATIONS, DESIGNED BY CHARLES McKIM IN THE EARLY 1900'S AND PARTLY MODELED AFTER A ROMAN BATH. BUT WAY BETTER, BECAUSE THOSE OLD ROMAN BATHS WERE JUST FULL OF NAKED ROMANS,

WHILE PENN STATION WAS FULL OF TRAINS: SLEEK STAINLESS STEEL TRAINS HIGHBALLING IN FROM THE HINTERLANDS. BACK IN 1967, THEY KNOCKED DOWN THE OLD STATION AND REPLACED IT WITH THE CURRENT ONE: A BIG HOLE IN THE GROUND WHERE COMMUTER TRAINS SKITTER AROUND LIKE FAT DUMPSTER RATS.

I SPEND THE NIGHT ON MY FRIEND'S COUCH IN BUSHWICK. WHEN I WAKE UP IN THE MORNING, IT'S WINDY. A COLD WIND FROM CANADA THAT BLOWS AWAY ALL THAT TALK OF AN EARLY SPRING. PUFFY CLOUDS, TATTERED AND TORN TO SHREDS, SCUD OVER THE CITY. LIKE THE REMNANTS OF SOME CLOUD MASSACRE THAT TOOK PLACE IN THE SKY WEST OF HERE, ABOVE INDIANA OR OHIO. AND HERE'S WHAT'S LEFT: CORPSE CLOUDS, DISMEMBERED AND DRIFTING DOWNWIND OVER

NEW YORK. "CORPSE CLOUDS?"
MY FRIEND IN BUSHWICK SAYS WHEN
I TELL HER WHAT I'M THINKING,
"THAT'S KIND OF FUCKED UP."

WHEN MY FRIEND GOES TO WORK,
I TAKE THE SUBWAY TO THE
VILLAGE AND I GET A SLICE OF
PIZZA AT THE KOSHER PIZZA
PLACE ON SECOND AVE. IT'S A
GOOD SLICE: VEGGIE SAUSAGE,
OLIVES, AND SOME CRUMBLED-UP
TOFU. IT'S GOOD, BUT IT'S NOT
AS GOOD AS I REMEMBER. NOTHING'S
EVER AS GOOD AS THAT. THIS
THOUGHT CHEERS ME UP. IT MEANS
THERE'S NOTHING TO GO BACK TO,
AND THERE'S NOTHING TO KEEP YOU
AROUND. IT MEANS THE NEXT
REALLY GOOD SLICE OF VEGAN
PIZZA IS SOMEWHERE ELSE, WAIT-
ING FOR YOU, AND THE ONLY THING
TO DO IS HIT THE ROAD AND GO
LOOKING FOR IT.

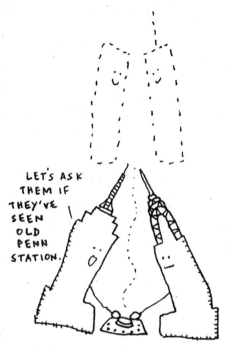

THE EMPIRE STATE AND THE CHRYSLER CONTACT THE TWINS WITH A OUIJA BOARD.

MONTREAL

THE WIND HAS STOPPED TAKING ITS
MEDS AGAIN. NOW IT'S OUT OF
ITS HEAD, WHIPPING THROUGH THE
STREETS AND SPINNING STRAY GUM
WRAPPERS AND CIGARETTE BUTTS
IN TIGHT CIRCLES. YESTERDAY WAS
SPRING, BUT TODAY IT'S WINTER
ALL OVER AGAIN. THE SUN IS OUT,
BUT IT'S GOT ALL THE WARM STUFF
DRAINED OUT OF IT. A BRIGHT
SUN THAT WON'T SAVE YOU FROM
THE COLD, BUT WILL ENSURE THAT
WHEREVER IT IS YOU FINALLY FREEZE
TO DEATH IS WELL-LIT.

THE TRAIN ROLLS NORTH OUT OF THE
CITY, AND THE WEATHER JUST KEEPS
GETTING COLDER. THE COUNTRY OUT-
SIDE LOOKS DENSE AND HARD, LIKE
ALL THE LITTLE ATOMS ARE HUDDLED
CLOSE, TRYING TO KEEP WARM.
THERE'S NOTHING DREAMY OR

SPECTRAL ABOUT THE ICE PLANET I'M ROLLING THROUGH. IT LOOKS HARD — A ROCK HARD FACT OF A WORLD IT'S NO USE ARGUING WITH. NOT THE SOFT, STEAMY GHOST WORLD OF MID-JULY, BUT A WORLD THAT'S LIKE A BLUNT OBJECT TO THE HEAD.

YESTERDAY, MY PAL AND I WATCHED THE OLD VETERAN'S STADIUM GET BLOWN TO SMITHEREENS. ACTUALLY, WE JUST MISSED THE IMPLOSION BECAUSE WE SLEPT TOO LATE. BY THE TIME WE GOT DOWN TO SOUTH PHILLY, THERE WAS JUST A BIG CLOUD OF DUST IN THE DISTANCE. THEN THE CLOUD DRIFTED AWAY AND THE STADIUM WAS GONE. THE STREETS WERE FULL OF PEOPLE WHO'D GOTTEN UP EARLY ON A SUNDAY MORNING TO WATCH THE SHOW; SOUTH PHILLY KIDS DRINKING FORTIES INSTEAD OF COFFEE AT 7 AM, AND

TURNING THE END OF THE STADIUM INTO A STREET PARTY. THIS MORNING, I SAID GOODBYE TO MY PAL WHO LIVES IN PHILLY. RESIGNED TO THE FACT THAT THERE'S NO USE STAYING. NO USE LOOKING FOR THE PERFECT LIFE THERE. IT'S WAY TOO MUCH TO ASK FOR, ANYWAY. A PERFECT LIFE. YOU'RE LUCKY IF YOU JUST GET A PERFECT MINUTE OR TWO.

WHEN THE TRAIN GETS TO MONTREAL, I GO TO A CAFE AND ASK FOR A CUP OF FENNEL TEA IN FRENCH. IT'S A DANGEROUS THING TO DO. ALL THE KIDS IN THIS TOWN SPEAK FRENCH AND ENGLISH, SO WHEN YOU TRY TO ACT COOL AND ASK FOR A CUP OF TEA IN FRENCH, SUDDENLY THE KID AT THE COUNTER IS ASKING YOU ALL SORTS OF QUESTIONS — DO YOU WANT IT TO STAY OR TO GO? DO YOU WANT THE

TEA BAG IN OR OUT? MY FRENCH
IS CRUMMY, SO I STARE AT THE KID
AT THE COUNTER, HELPLESS AND
STUPID, TILL SHE RESCUES ME BY
SPEAKING ENGLISH. SECRETLY, I
LOVE THIS LANGUAGE TORTURE,
AND I LOVE HOW IT GOES BOTH
WAYS. FOR INSTANCE, WHEN YOU
WALK INTO A CAFE IN MONTREAL,
THE PERSON AT THE COUNTER
HAS TO FIGURE OUT WHAT LANGUAGE
TO GREET YOU IN. SOMETIMES,
THEY'LL SPLIT THE DIFFERENCE, AND
SAY SOMETHING LIKE "BONJOUR,
HELLO." THEN THEY WAIT FOR YOU
TO SAY SOMETHING, WHICH IMMED-
IATELY CLEARS EVERYTHING UP.
BUT OTHER TIMES, YOU'LL WALK
INTO A PLACE, AND THE PERSON
AT THE COUNTER WILL PROFILE
YOU. THEN THEY'LL START
TALKING TO YOU IN ENGLISH OR
IN FRENCH, DEPENDING ON THEIR
CONCLUSIONS. WHAT SURPRISES ME

IS HOW OFTEN THEY'RE WRONG, AND THEY'LL START TALKING TO ME IN FRENCH. IS IT BECAUSE I WEAR FUNNY GLASSES? OR DO THEY MISTAKE MY QUIET TERROR OF MAKING A FOOL OUT OF MYSELF FOR SOME KIND OF FRANCOPHONE INTENSITY? MAYBE PEOPLE IN MONTREAL WOULD DISAGREE, BUT I THINK ALL THESE LANGUAGE HASSLES ARE THE BEST THING ABOUT THE PLACE: ALL THESE MILLION MOMENTS OF AWKWARD-NESS AS PEOPLE WHO LIVE IN THE SAME CITY TRY TO FIGURE OUT HOW TO SAY HELLO TO EACH OTHER.

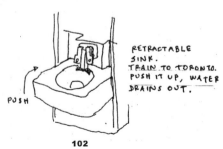

PUSH

RETRACTABLE SINK. TRAIN TO TORONTO. PUSH IT UP, WATER DRAINS OUT.

Village Inn
MOTEL
FREE HBO

RATON, N.M.
7/05

TERROR.

WHAT MAKES TERRORISTS SO
TERRIFYING THESE DAYS IS THAT
THEY'RE STARTING TO ACT LIKE
GLOBAL CAPITALISTS. THEY'VE
TURNED FEAR INTO A FRANCHISE.
ALL IT TAKES IS A BOMB OR AN
ASSAULT RIFLE AND — BAM! —
YOU'RE A FRANCHISEE, SERVING
UP MISERY THE WAY BURGER KING
SERVES WHOPPERS. I HATE THE
TERRORISTS, NOT LEAST OF ALL
BECAUSE THEY TARGET EVERYTHING
I LIKE BEST: TRAINS AND SKY-
SCRAPERS AND SUBWAYS LIKE THIS
ONE, THE ONE I'M RIDING UNDER
MONTREAL. AT THE LUCIEN
L'ALLIER STOP, THE CAR FILLS
UP WITH A BUNCH OF LITTLE
KIDS — 3RD OR 4TH GRADERS ON A
FIELD TRIP. I CLOSE MY EYES
AND LISTEN TO THE STEADY ROAR

OF THE TRAIN, AND OVER THAT,
THE SOUND OF A SUBWAY CAR
FULL OF LITTLE KIDS CHATTERING
IN FRENCH. AND FOR A MOMENT,
I FEEL SAFE. LIKE, FOR THIS
MOMENT, I'M BEYOND THE REACH
OF TERRIBLE THINGS. FOR AS
LONG AS THESE LITTLE KIDS KEEP
LAUGHING AND THIS TRAIN KEEPS
ROLLING.

HEY!

Did you used to do Food Not Bombs in Pilson? (I have an alarmingly good memory for FACES).

P.S. John Kerry just announced he was going to concede. (F.Y.I.) ☺

ATOMIX COFFEE.
CHICAGO.

FREIGHT SHIP.

MY CABIN HAS A BED AND A COUCH
AND A COFFEE TABLE THAT'S
BOLTED TO THE FLOOR. THOSE
BOLTS WORRY ME. THEY MEAN
THERE ARE DAYS ON THIS SHIP
WHEN THE FURNITURE NEEDS
BOLTING DOWN. I SLEPT ON THE
COUCH LAST NIGHT. MAYBE OUT
OF HABIT. MAYBE BECAUSE I'M
MORE COMFORTABLE ON COUCHES.
WHEN YOU SLEEP IN A BED, YOU
HAVE RESPONSIBILITIES. THERE
ARE SHEETS TO PULL DOWN AND
PILLOWS TO PROP UP, AND SOME-
TIMES THERE ARE OTHER PEOPLE,
TOO. A BED IS FOR SLEEPING,
BUT A COUCH IS FOR SLEEPING
AROUND. I CONSIDER SLEEPING ON
THE COUCH EVERY NIGHT, LIKE
I'M COUCH SURFING ACROSS THE

107

ATLANTIC OCEAN. THAT'S A COUCH
SURFER'S DREAM. AFTER ALL: CATCHING
A RIDE ON SOME COUCH THAT'LL
TAKE YOU AROUND THE WORLD; LIKE
SOME SLACKER MAGELLAN, MOOCHING
A CIRCUMNAVIGATION.

BREAKFAST ON THE SHIP LASTS FROM
07:30 TO 08:30. MY TABLE IS IN
THE OFFICER'S MESS. I'M THE
ONLY PASSENGER, SO I SIT AT A
BIG TABLE ALL ALONE. THE
CAPTAIN SITS AT A TABLE NEXT
TO MINE. HE'S AN INDIAN GUY WITH
A BUSHY GRAY MUSTACHE AND A
BIG BELLY. HE TELLS ME HE'S BEEN
AT SEA SINCE 1964. I SHAKE MY
HEAD AT THE THOUGHT OF IT. 40
YEARS FLOATING ON WATER.
THERE'S A LOT OF SEA IN THIS
GUY. I ASK THE CAPTAIN ABOUT
MY BOLTED-DOWN COFFEE TABLE.
HE SHRUGS. "IT'S THE ATLANTIC.

IT GETS ROUGH. "

JUST BEFORE BREAKFAST ENDS, THE PILOT SHOWS UP. HE'S A FRENCH-CANADIAN GUY WHO ORDERS A HUGE BREAKFAST: EGGS, TOAST, POTATOES, COFFEE. THE STEWARD OFFERS HIM SOME MANGO JUICE, BUT THE PILOT MAKES A FACE AND ASKS FOR ORANGE JUICE INSTEAD. THE PILOT TELLS ME HE'S FROM MONTREAL, AND HIS JOB IS TO GUIDE THE SHIP DOWN THE ST. LAWRENCE RIVER AS FAR AS THE TOWN OF TROIS-RIVIERES. THAT'S WHERE HE HOPS OFF AND ANOTHER PILOT TAKES OVER. IT TAKES A TOTAL OF THREE PILOTS TO GUIDE A FREIGHT SHIP TO THE MOUTH OF THE ST. LAWRENCE. THEN WE'RE ON OUR OWN.

LATER ON, I'LL NOTICE THAT EVERY TIME A NEW PILOT COMES

ABOARD, THE FIRST THING HE'LL DO IS EAT A BIG MEAL COMPLIMENTS OF THE SHIP. IT'S A LITTLE TRADITION, I GUESS. A FORM OF NAUTICAL HOSPITALITY THAT MAKES ME SMILE. SURE, PILOTING A 60,000 TON FREIGHT SHIP DOWN A BUSY RIVER IS SERIOUS BUSINESS, BUT THAT DOESN'T MEAN IT CAN'T WAIT TILL THE PILOT HAS A BITE TO EAT.

MANGO JUICE AND BLACK TEA.

MOST OF THE CREW IS FROM INDIA, SO WHEN IT COMES TO MEALS, THIS SHIP IS AN ENORMOUS FLOATING INDIAN RESTAURANT. DAL AND PAPPANAN AND ALOO GOBI. MANGO JUICE, KEIR, AND BLACK TEA. IT'S A GOOD SHIP TO BE A VEGETARIAN ON. IF THIS WERE A GERMAN SHIP, IT'D BE ALL WURSTS AND SCHNITZEL, AND I'D STARVE TO DEATH. AT SEA, TIME TURNS CELESTIAL. IT'S DAY WHEN THE SUN'S UP, AND IT'S NIGHT WHEN THERE ARE STARS. IF THE SKY IS OVERCAST, THERE'S NO TIME AT ALL. THERE IS JUST A TERRIBLE TIMELESS VOID THAT THE SHIP BOBS IN THE MIDDLE OF. MAYBE THAT'S WHY MEALS ARE SUCH A BIG DEAL : BREAKFAST AT 07:30

SHARP, AND LUNCH AT 12:00, AND
DINNER AT 18:30. SEA TIME MAY
BE CELESTIAL, BUT MEAL TIME IS
MAN-MADE; IT'S A LINK TO THAT
TIME WE LEFT BEHIND, WAY
BACK ON SHORE.

AT LUNCH, THE CAPTAIN TELLS ME
ABOUT INTERNATIONAL TRADE.
"IT CAN BE SUMMED UP LIKE THIS,"
HE SAYS. "THE U.S. IMPORTS
ATHLETIC SHOES AND EXPORTS
WEAPONS." WHEN HE SAYS THIS,
I GET A CHILL. LIKE THAT'S
THE AWFUL SECRET; THE
SECRET ORDER OF THINGS HIDDEN
INSIDE ALL THOSE ANONYMOUS
FREIGHT CONTAINERS STACKED
UP ON DECK. THE CAPTAIN TELLS
ME OUR SHIP, THE CAST PROSPECT,
USED TO BE CALLED THE CANMAR
FORTUNE. IN THE OLD DAYS, CAST
AND CANMAR WERE INDEPENDENT

SHIPPING LINES. BUT FOLLOWING A PERIOD OF MERGERS AND CONSOLIDATIONS, BOTH LINES ARE NOW OWNED BY SOME GIANT PARENT COMPANY WHICH KEEPS THE OLD NAMES ALIVE FOR THE SAME REASON PABST STILL BOTTLES OLYMPIA AND OLD STYLE: BECAUSE CORPORATIONS MAY NOT BE LOYAL OR SENTIMENTAL, BUT PEOPLE ARE.

AFTER LUNCH, I HEAD UP TO THE BRIDGE TO SEE WHAT'S GOING ON UP THERE. THE CAPTAIN TELLS ME I'M WELCOME ON THE BRIDGE, BUT THAT IT'S A BUSY PLACE AND THAT HE DOESN'T HAVE TIME TO ANSWER ANY QUESTIONS. THEN HE MAKES ME A CUP OF STRONG BLACK TEA WITH SUGAR AND CONDENSED MILK, AND HE PROCEEDS TO ANSWER ALL MY QUESTIONS. HE TELLS ME THE SHIP IS CRUISING

AT 12 KNOTS RIGHT NOW. IT CAN GET UP TO 21 KNOTS, BUT IT NEVER GOES THAT FAST BECAUSE THE SEA IS USUALLY TOO ROUGH. HE POINTS OUT THE RADAR AND THE SATELLITE PHONE AND THE G.P.S., AND HE INTRODUCES ME TO THE HELMSMAN WHO'S WEARING A NEON-ORANGE JUMPSUIT AND WHO STANDS IN FRONT OF A LITTLE PLASTIC STEERING WHEEL THAT LOOKS LIKE IT CAME OFF AN OLD ARCADE VIDEO GAME MACHINE. "POLE POSITION," MAYBE. THE CAPTAIN ASKS ME IF I LIKE THE TEA. I TELL HIM IT'S GOOD BUT STRONG. HE SAYS IT'S CALLED "500-MILE TEA", BECAUSE THAT'S HOW LONG A CUP OF IT WILL KEEP YOU AWAKE. "LIVERPOOL IS STILL 8 OR 9 CUPS AWAY," HE SAYS WITH A SMILE. FINALLY, THE

CAPTAIN EXCUSES HIMSELF. THEN
THE BRIDGE GOES QUIET,
EXCEPT FOR THE OCCASIONAL
SQUAWK OF THE RADIO, AND THE
RASPY SOUND OF ICE FLOES
SCRAPING AGAINST THE STEEL
HULL.

COLUMBUS, OH.

THE BRIDGE.

I KEEP DREAMING ABOUT BUILDINGS.
MAYBE IT'S BECAUSE I WON'T SEE
ANY FOR A WHOLE WEEK. I DREAM
ABOUT BUILDINGS AND THE BRIDGES
BETWEEN BUILDINGS. NOT THOSE
1970'S PEDESTRIAN BRIDGES YOU
FIND AT AIRPORTS AND SHOPPING
MALLS THAT LOOK LIKE GIANT
HAMSTER TUBES, BUT OLD FASHIONED
BRIDGES, WAY UP HIGH, CONNECTING
ONE GOTHIC-REVIVAL SKYSCRAPER
TO ANOTHER. THERE ARE LONG
HALLWAYS IN MY DREAMS,
AND LINOLEUM FLOORS GLOSSED
WITH A MILLION COATS OF WAX.
THERE ARE OLD OFFICE DOORS SET
WITH BUBBLED GLASS, AND THE
SILHOUETTES OF THE PEOPLE BEHIND
THE GLASS DON'T MOVE, EXACTLY,
BUT CLEAVE; SHADOWY FORMS
THAT BUBBLE AND BILLOW LIKE

THOSE BLOBS IN A LAVA LAMP.
MAYBE I'M DREAMING THIS STUFF
BECAUSE THERE ARE NO BUILDINGS
AT SEA, THERE'S JUST THE SHIP.
AND THERE ARE NO BRIDGES,
THERE'S JUST THE BRIDGE. THE
BRIDGE, IT TURNS OUT, IS MOSTLY
EMPTY. I THOUGHT IT'D BE LIKE
THE COCKPIT OF A JET PLANE,
OR EVEN LIKE THE BRIDGE ON THE
STARSHIP ENTERPRISE, PACKED
TIGHT WITH INSTRUMENTS.
INSTEAD, THERE ARE JUST THREE
TABLES WITH A FEW BUTTONS
AND SCOPES ARRANGED IN A U-
SHAPE IN THE MIDDLE OF THE
ROOM. IT LOOKS UNCONVINCING,
THE BRIDGE. LIKE A SET CON-
STRUCTED BY A JUNIOR HIGH DRAMA
CLUB FOR THEIR UPDATED VERSION
OF MOBY DICK. THE WEIRDEST
THING IS THAT THERE AREN'T
EVEN ANY CHAIRS ON THE BRIDGE.

ISN'T THERE SUPPOSED TO BE A CAPTAIN'S SEAT? A PLUSH SWIVEL SEAT WITH ARMRESTS THAT THE CAPTAIN CAN BARK COMMANDS FROM? A CORPORATE C.E.O. HAS A BIG LEATHER CHAIR, AND A MOVIE DIRECTOR HAS A DIRECTOR'S CHAIR, AND OF COURSE A KING HAS A THRONE. BUT ON THE BRIDGE, THERE'S NO PLACE FOR THE CAPTAIN TO SIT. INSTEAD, HE LOITERS AROUND THE CONTROL CONSOLES, LOOKING A BIT AWKWARD AND UNCOMFORTABLE. THEN HE WANDERS OVER TO THE ELECTRIC KETTLE AND BOILS SOME WATER FOR A CUP OF TEA. FINALLY, HE HEADS BACK TO HIS OFFICE TO DO HIS PAPERWORK. HE TELLS ME THAT'S REALLY WHAT HIS JOB IS ABOUT. THE COMPUTERS TAKE CARE OF THE SAILING, AND HE DOES THE PAPERWORK.

THE 3RD OFFICER.

THE SHIP HAS A PASSENGER'S LOUNGE.
SINCE I'M THE ONLY PASSENGER, I
HAVE IT TO MYSELF. IT HAS AN
EXERCISE BIKE, AND SOME COUCHES,
AND A SMALL COLLECTION OF OLD
BRITISH COMEDIES ON VIDEO TAPE:
"FAWLTY TOWERS" AND "DAD'S
ARMY" AND "ARE YOU BEING
SERVED?" WHEN I WAS A LITTLE
KID BACK IN TEXAS, THE LOCAL
PBS STATION WOULD PLAY THOSE
SHOWS LATE ON SATURDAY NIGHT.
SOMETIMES I'D SNEAK DOWN TO
THE TV AND WATCH THEM WITH
THE VOLUME TURNED LOW. I
REMEMBER I DIDN'T UNDERSTAND
MOST OF THE JOKES, BUT I LIKED
THE SHOWS BECAUSE THEY WEREN'T
LIKE ANYTHING I'D EVER SEEN
BEFORE. IT WAS LIKE WATCHING
TV BEAMED FROM AN ALIEN

PLANET.

ALONG ONE WALL OF THE PASSENGER'S LOUNGE, THERE'S A ROW OF WINDOWS THAT LOOK OUT ONTO THE BOW OF THE SHIP. EVERY NIGHT, THE STEWARD COMES BY AND CLOSES THE CURTAINS OVER THE WINDOWS. TACKED TO THE WALL, THERE'S EVEN A SIGN THAT ASKS YOU TO PLEASE KEEP THE CURTAINS CLOSED AT NIGHT. IT DOESN'T EXPLAIN WHY. THE LOUNGE IS ON DECK FOUR, HIGH ABOVE THE REST OF THE SHIP, SO IT ISN'T A MATTER OF PRIVACY. I FIGURE IT MIGHT BE ANOTHER ONE OF THOSE NAUTICAL TRADITIONS, LIKE NAMING SHIPS AFTER WOMEN, OR NOT SETTING SAIL ON A FRIDAY. OR MAYBE IT'S FOR PSYCHOLOGICAL REASONS. NIGHTTIME AT SEA IS SCARY. IT'S PITCH BLACK. A VAST, EMPTY BLACKNESS THAT ANYTHING COULD COME OUT OF: TIDAL WAVES

OR SEA MONSTERS OR THE GHOSTS
OF DROWNED PIRATES. BETTER TO
KEEP THE CURTAINS CLOSED. THEY
WON'T PROTECT YOU FROM THE
TERRORS OF THE SEA, BUT AT
LEAST THEY'LL HELP YOU FORGET
ABOUT THEM.

A FEW DAYS AFTER WE SET SAIL,
I MEET THE 3RD OFFICER IN THE
PASSENGER'S LOUNGE FOR THE
MANDATORY SAFETY LECTURE.
HE TELLS ME ABOUT THE LIFE
VESTS AND THE LIFE BOATS,
AND HOW IF THE SHIP'S HORN
STARTS BLOWING REPEATEDLY, I
SHOULD PUT ON THE ONE AND RUN
FOR THE OTHER. HE ALSO TELLS
ME THAT THE PASSENGER'S
LOUNGE IS JUST A COUPLE DECKS
BELOW THE BRIDGE, AND AT NIGHT
I SHOULD KEEP THE CURTAINS
SHUT. THAT WAY, THE LIGHT
FROM THE LOUNGE WON'T LEAK OUT

THE WINDOWS AND INTERFERE WITH THE NIGHT-VISION INSTRUMENTS UP THERE. NO PROBLEM, I TELL THE 3RD OFFICER. I PREFER THE CURTAINS SHUT.

Piracy has come a long way since the days of the cutlass and galleon.

Modern pirates are armed with speedboats, AK-47's and mobile phones.

In a typical attack at least 10 men in high-speed launch will follow a freighter, on which an insider has usually been planted beforehand to provide location and freight details.

> **"** Modern piracy is made all the more fearless because its victims know they are alone and defenceless **"**
>
> Jayant Abhyankar

Once boarded they will either hijack the ship for its cargo, or, more typically, go straight to the captain's safe, which usually contains tens of thousands of dollars in petty cash.

Sometimes the ship is repainted and given a new name, and false documents are used to create a new identity for the vessel.

Entire crews have also been known to have been kidnapped or murdered.

Last December the Chinese authorities executed 13 Chinese pirates who had been convicted of murdering 23 crew members of the cargo ship Cheung Son, which was seized just outside Hong Kong waters by pirates dressed as Chinese officials.

The South China Sea is considered the most dangerous for piracy in the world.

About half of the record 285 attacks recorded by the International Maritime Bureau (IMB) last year occurred here, with Indonesia and Malaysia among the worst-hit nations.

Jayant Abhyankar, the deputy director of the IMB, told The Daily Telegraph newspaper that the increase "highlights that modern piracy is violent, bloody and ruthless".

The IMB reported that pirates world-wide in 1999 carried guns on 53 occasions and knives were used twice as often as the previous year.

Gun-battles

Approximately one-third of the world's commercial shipping passes through the South China Sea annually.

Some coastal towns in Malaysia's Sabah state, the scene of Sunday's tourist kidnappings, have been regularly targeted by armed Filipino gangs.

In September 1998, a group of armed pirates killed a fisherman in Bohayan Island in Sabah, took his boat and robbed other fishermen.

Photographs showing the drunken pirates celebrating the killing spree were later found by police, although the ship was never found.

The IMB's advice to ships which are being followed is to sail full speed ahead and radio for help.

It urges ships to maintain constant anti-piracy watches, even when in port.

WAVES V. SWELLS

WAVES ARE CAUSED BY THE WIND.
ONCE THE WIND DIES DOWN, SO
DO THE WAVES. BUT SWELLS ARE
SOMETHING ELSE, SOME MARITIME
BLACK MAGIC CONJURED UP BY
NAIADS AND SEA NYMPHS. JUST
OFF NEWFOUNDLAND, THE SHIP
STARTS TO PITCH, WHICH IS WHAT
A SHIP DOES WHEN IT HITS A
SWELL HEAD-ON. MY LITTLE
TRAVEL ALARM CLOCK SAYS IT'S
10:42 AM, TEXAS TIME, A TIME
ZONE WE'RE SAILING FARTHER
AND FARTHER AHEAD OF. ON
THE SHIP, IT'S 2:42 PM. IT'LL
TAKE 4 HOURS EXACTLY FOR THIS
VERY SAME MOMENT TO DRIFT
BACK OVER TEXAS, LIKE THE
QUIETEST KIND OF BREEZE. BUT
FOR NOW, 2:42 PM IS HERE,
HOVERING OVER THE HIGH SEAS

JUST OFF THE CONTINENTAL SHELF.

I SPEND MOST OF THE MORNING ON
THE BRIDGE, WATCHING THE
CAPTAIN AND THE 3RD OFFICER
TAKING APART ONE OF THE CONTROL
CONSOLES. THEY'RE TRYING TO
FIND A SQUEAK IN THE THING, A
LITTLE EEK-EEK NOISE SET OFF
BY THE VIBRATION OF THE SHIP'S
ENGINE. AFTER A FEW DAYS AT
SEA, A LITTLE SQUEAK LIKE THAT
CAN DRIVE YOU NUTS. IT FILLS
THE SPACIOUS VOID YOU'RE SAILING
THROUGH TILL IT'S EVERYTHING,
THAT ANNOYING SQUEAK, AS
BIG AS THE SKY AND THE SEA.
WHEN THE CAPTAIN AND THE 3RD
OFFICER REASSEMBLE THE CONSOLE,
THE SQUEAK IS STILL THERE. SO
THEY BREAK THE THING DOWN
AND START OVER AGAIN.
AT 16:30, THERE'S A FIRE DRILL.

I STAND IN THE HALLWAY IN FRONT OF MY CABIN WEARING A NEON ORANGE LIFE JACKET AND A WHITE HARDHAT THAT'S GOT "PASSENGER" WRITTEN ON IT IN BLACK MARKER. I STAND THERE, WAITING FOR THE ALARM AND SMILING TO MYSELF BECAUSE THIS IS CERTAINLY NOT WHAT A REAL EMERGENCY WOULD BE LIKE: SCHEDULED AT A PRECISE TIME ON A SUNNY DAY OVER CALM SEAS. AT 16:30:00, THE ALARM SOUNDS. THE 3RD OFFICER LEADS ME TO THE STARBOARD LIFEBOAT. WE CLIMB ABOARD. THE LIFEBOAT IS COMPLETELY ENCLOSED IN A FIBERGLASS SHELL. INSIDE, IT SMELLS LIKE DIESEL FUEL AND TAR. THE 3RD OFFICER GIVES ME A CRASH COURSE IN LIFEBOAT OPERATIONS, IN THE HOPEFULLY

UNLIKELY AND TOTALLY NIGHT-
MARISH EVENT THAT I HAVE TO
SINGLE-HANDEDLY LAUNCH THE
BOAT AND DRIVE IT AWAY FROM
THE BURNING AND/OR SINKING
SHIP. AFTER THE LESSON IS
OVER, I DON'T HAVE THE SLIGHT-
EST IDEA HOW TO LAUNCH A
LIFEBOAT, BUT I DO
LEARN THAT IF SOMETHING
BAD HAPPENS TO THE SHIP, I'M
DOOMED. AS THE 3RD OFFICER
AND I CLIMB THE STAIRS BACK
TO THE BRIDGE, WE PASS THE
EXHAUST FAN FROM THE SHIP'S
GALLEY. THE SMELL OF INDIAN
FOOD COOKING INSIDE IS COMFORT-
ING AFTER ALL THIS DISASTER
DRILLING. I CAN ONLY HOPE THE
LIFEBOATS ARE WELL-PROVISIONED
WITH AN EMERGENCY SUPPLY OF
VEGETABLE SAMOSAS AND TAMARIND
SAUCE, IN ADDITION TO THE RESCUE
FLARES AND THE RADIO BEACONS.

WHEN YOU'RE TRYING TO SINGLE-
HANDEDLY LAUNCH A LIFEBOAT
FROM A LISTING SHIP IN STORMY
SEAS, I BET A VEGETABLE
SAMOSA SURE HITS THE SPOT.

MINNEAPOLIS, MN.

THE FLEMISH CAP

ONE DAY ON THE BRIDGE, THE 3RD
OFFICER EXPLAINS TO ME HOW
THINGS WORK. THE SHIP WE'RE
ON IS OWNED BY CANADIAN
PACIFIC, THE HUGE CONGLOMERATE
THAT OWNS THE CP RAILROAD AND
LOTS OF OTHER STUFF. CP
CONTRACTS A COMPANY IN
INDIA CALLED ANGLO-EASTERN
TO PROVIDE A CREW FOR THE
SHIP. THAT'S WHY ALL THE
OFFICERS AND MOST OF THE
REGULAR SEAMEN ARE INDIAN.
WHEN A SAILOR IS HIRED, HE SIGNS
A 6 OR 7 MONTH CONTRACT,
WHICH MEANS HE'LL BE ON THE
SHIP PRETTY MUCH NON-STOP FOR
6 OR 7 MONTHS. AFTER HIS
CONTRACT ENDS, HE USUALLY
HEADS HOME FOR A WHILE BEFORE
SIGNING A NEW CONTRACT. THE

3RD OFFICER TELLS ME THAT IN ADDITION TO INDIANS, THERE ARE PHILIPPINOS AND A FEW SAMOANS WORKING ON THE SHIP, TOO. HE SAYS THE INDIAN SAILORS ARE GOOD AT SAVING MONEY, BUT PHILIPPINO SAILORS BLOW ALL THEIR CASH IN PORT. AND DON'T EVEN ASK ABOUT THE SAMOANS. THE 3RD OFFICER IS KIND OF A SNOB. SO IS THE 2ND OFFICER, A CHUBBY GUY WHO'S IN CHARGE OF NAVIGATION AND WHO'S A REAL KNOW-IT-ALL. I DON'T EXACTLY TRUST THE 2ND OFFICER. HE SEEMS LIKE THE KIND OF GUY WHO, IF THE SHIP WERE SINKING, WOULD HOP INTO A LIFEBOAT AND LEAVE THE REST OF US BEHIND. I LIKE THE FIRST MATE, THOUGH. HE'S A YOUNG GUY WHO LIVED IN THE U.K. FOR A WHILE. HE EVEN ADOPTED AN ENGLISH NAME:

NICKY ANDREW. NICKY TELLS ME.
HE WANTS TO BE A SHIP'S CAPTAIN
SOMEDAY. HE TELLS ME HE
WANTS TO SEE THE WORLD. NICKY
SEEMS TO BE A LITTLE BIT OF AN
OUTCAST. THE OTHER OFFICERS
DON'T JOKE WITH HIM THE WAY
THEY JOKE WITH EACH OTHER.
MAYBE IT'S PARTLY TO DO WITH
THE NAME CHANGE AND THE
ANGLOPHILIA. IT MAKES ME
WONDER IF INDIAN PEOPLE HAVE
A NAME FOR THAT — FOR SOMEONE
WHO IS INDIAN ON THE OUTSIDE
BUT ENGLISH ON THE INSIDE.

LIKE I SAY, THE 3RD OFFICER IS A
SNOB, BUT HE'S OKAY. WHEN THE
CAPTAIN IS AWAY AND THE 3RD OFFICER
IS ALONE ON THE BRIDGE, HE
GETS PRETTY CHATTY. HE TELLS
ME ABOUT THE EXAMS HE HAS TO
TAKE TO ADVANCE IN RANK; AND

HE TELLS ME THAT ICEBERGS ARE
JUST AS DANGEROUS AS THEY'VE
ALWAYS BEEN BECAUSE THE RADAR
CAN'T ALWAYS SPOT THEM; AND
HE POINTS OUT THE LITTLE GREEN
DOTS ON THE RADAR THAT ARE
FISHING BOATS BOBBING ABOVE
THE FLEMISH CAP. THE CAP IS A
HIGH SPOT ON THE OCEAN FLOOR
WHERE THE FISHING IS GOOD. IT'S
A TRICKY SPOT, THOUGH. THE
SEA ABOVE THE CAP CAN GET
ROUGH IN A HURRY. "EVER SEE
THE MOVIE "THE PERFECT STORM?"
HE ASKS ME. "THIS IS IT. PERFECT
STORM COUNTRY."

I ASK THE 3RD OFFICER IF SHIPS
EXCHANGE SOME KIND OF MARITIME
GREETING WHEN THEY PASS EACH
OTHER ON THE HIGH SEAS, THE
WAY FARMERS IN WEST TEXAS
RAISE A SINGLE FINGER OFF THEIR
STEERING WHEELS AS A SORT OF
SILENT "HOWDY-DO" WHEN THEY

DRIVE PAST ONE ANOTHER ON A
COUNTRY ROAD. AFTER ALL,
THE NORTH ATLANTIC LOOKS
A LOT LIKE WEST TEXAS, ALL
WIDE-OPEN AND LONESOME. BUT
THE 3RD OFFICER TELLS ME THAT
SHIPS USUALLY JUST PASS EACH
OTHER IN SILENCE.

TUCSON, AZ.

TUCSON.

THE FIRST MATE.

ON THE FOURTH DAY OUT AT SEA,
THE FIRST MATE — OFFICIALLY,
HE'S CALLED THE CHIEF OFFICER —
TAKES ME ON A TOUR OF THE SHIP.
IT'S A NICE THING FOR HIM TO
DO, CONSIDERING HOW BUSY HE IS.
THESE FREIGHT SHIPS — JUST LIKE
A WALMART OR A McDONALD'S —
KEEP CREW TO AN ABSOLUTE
MINIMUM, SO ALL THE SAILORS
ARE REALLY BUSY. WHEN THEY'RE
NOT WORKING, THEY'RE USUALLY
CATCHING UP ON SOME SLEEP.
NICKY TAKES ME OUT ON DECK
WHERE THE GIANT FREIGHT CON-
TAINERS ARE STACKED FIVE HIGH,
AND HE TAKES ME TO THE ENGINE
ROOM AND SHOWS ME THE
SEVEN-PISTON GODZILLA-SIZED
ENGINE. THE ENGINE ROOM IS
LOUD. DEAFENING, IN FACT. LIKE
AN EXPERIMENTAL GERMAN

NOISE BAND ROCKING AT FULL VOLUME. THE ENGINE AND THE ANCHORS AND THE CARGO CONTAINERS ARE ALL VERY IMPRESSIVE, BUT MY FAVORITE PART OF THE TOUR IS A LITTLE COMPASS NEEDLE MOUNTED ON THE WALL IN NICKY'S OFFICE. THE COMPASS NEEDLE SHOWS YOU HOW MANY DEGREES THE SHIP IS ROLLING: THE ANGLE OF DEFLECTION. TODAY, IT'S MEASURING 5-DEGREES, WHICH IS NOTHING. IN ROUGH SEAS, THE SHIP CAN ROCK 30-DEGREES OR MORE. THAT'S WHEN IT'S HARD TO STAND UP. THE MORE THE SHIP ROLLS, THE MORE DANGER THERE IS THAT A FREIGHT CONTAINER WILL BREAK LOOSE AND TOPPLE OVERBOARD. THE CHIEF OFFICER'S MAIN JOB IS TO LOOK AFTER THE FREIGHT CONTAINERS, AND IF HE LOSES ONE, HE CAN KISS HIS JOB GOODBYE.

NICKY TELLS ME HE'S NEVER LOST A CONTAINER, BUT HE'S DEFINITELY HEARD ABOUT IT HAPPENING ON OTHER SHIPS. SOMETIMES, THE CONTAINERS WILL BREAK OPEN. THEN THOUSANDS OF PAIRS OF NIKE SNEAKERS OR GAP JEANS OR SONY DV-TAPES WILL FLOAT ON THE SURFACE OF THE OCEAN LIKE AN OIL SLICK.

THE NEXT DAY, WE RUN INTO SOME SWELLS. A 15-DEGREE DEFLECTION, NICKY SAYS. THE SHIP ROCKS BACK AND FORTH, SO I STAGGER DOWN THE HALLWAYS, KEEPING ONE HAND AGAINST THE WALL FOR BALANCE AND FEELING DRUNK ON THE MOTION. LATER, ON THE BRIDGE, NICKY EXPLAINS TO ME THAT THERE'S A WHOLE INVISIBLE TOPOGRAPHY ON THE SEA FLOOR THAT'S CHARTED AND

NAMED : UNDERSEA MOUNTAIN
RANGES AND VALLEYS AND
TRENCHES TOO DEEP TO MEASURE.
A WORLD NOT SO DIFFERENT FROM
THE WORLD WE LIVE ON, EXCEPT
THE SKY IS MADE OF WATER
INSTEAD OF AIR. BUT THE
SURFACE OF THE OCEAN IS A
DIFFERENT MATTER. THE SURFACE
ISN'T CHARTED OUT LIKE THAT.
BY DAY, IT'S FLAT BLUE AND
BLANK. BY NIGHT, IT TURNS
INTO A BLACK VOID THAT MAKES
OUTER SPACE SEEM CHEERY AND
BRIGHT BY COMPARISON. AT
LEAST EVEN THE DARKEST NIGHT
SKY HAS ITS STARS. BUT
EXCEPT FOR A LUMINESCENT
JELLY FISH OR TWO, THE SEA'S
GOT NOTHING AT ALL.
NICKY WAVES ME OVER TO THE
RADAR SCOPE AND POINTS OUT
A FUZZY GREEN ECHO. HE TELLS
ME IT'S PROBABLY A FREIGHT

SHIP. HE GRABS HIS BINOCULARS AND SCANS THE HORIZON. IT TAKES HIM A WHILE TO FIND IT. "SHIP AHOY!" HE FINALLY CALLS OUT. THEN HE LAUGHS. A LAUGH THAT SUMS THINGS UP. NOWADAYS, RADAR ANTENNAS MAN THE CROW'S NEST, AND SATELLITES DO THE STEERING, AND THE ONLY TIME YOU YELL "SHIP AHOY" IS WHEN YOU'RE MAKING A JOKE, SINCE THE RADAR ALWAYS SPOTS DISTANT SHIPS LONG BEFORE YOU CAN. ON A FREIGHT SHIP, THE CREW ARE CRANE OPERATORS OR COMPUTER TECHNICIANS OR MECHANICAL ENGINEERS. THEY'RE ONLY INCIDENTALLY SAILORS.

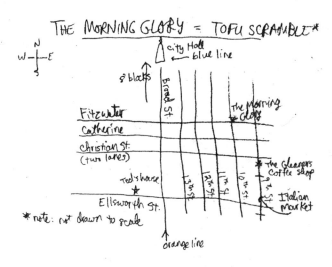

THE MORNING GLORY = TOFU SCRAMBLE*

TED'S MAP.
PHILLY.

SHIP TIME.

IN A CASINO, CLOCKS ARE JUST A
DISTRACTION FROM THE GAMBLING.
THAT'S WHY THERE ARE NEVER ANY
CLOCKS THERE. YOU'RE SUPPOSED
TO LOSE TRACK OF THE TIME, AND
BEFORE YOU KNOW IT, THE SUN IS
COMING UP AND YOU'VE STUCK
YOUR RETIREMENT SAVINGS INTO
A SLOT MACHINE, ONE QUARTER
AT A TIME. A FREIGHT SHIP IS
THE OPPOSITE OF A CASINO.
THERE ARE CLOCKS EVERYWHERE.
WHEN YOU'RE FLOATING IN THE
MIDDLE OF THE OCEAN, THEY KEEP
YOU FROM GOING CRAZY. THE
CLOCKS PARCEL OUT TIME IN
FAMILIAR MINUTES AND HOURS.
A COMFORTABLE SCALE. A SCALE
YOU CAN DEAL WITH. IF IT WEREN'T
FOR THE CLOCKS, THERE'D ONLY
BE OCEAN TIME, VAST AND WIDE
AND ALWAYS THREATENING TO SWELL

UP AND WASH YOU OVERBOARD. THERE
ARE CLOCKS IN THE CABINS, AND
CLOCKS IN THE LOUNGE, AND
CLOCKS IN THE MESS HALL. THEY'RE
ON EVERY LANDING AS YOU WALK
UP THE STAIRS FROM ONE DECK
TO ANOTHER. A COMPUTER CON-
TROLS THE CLOCKS AND CONSTANTLY
RESETS THEM, SHEDDING HOURS AS
YOU'RE SAILING EAST, AND
GATHERING THEM UP AGAIN AS YOU
SAIL WEST. IT'S SCARY WHEN
YOU SAIL OUT OF SIGHT OF THE
SHORE. ON THE OPEN SEA, EVEN
THE SUN LOOKS STRANGE, LIKE
MAYBE IT'S A DIFFERENT STAR
THAN THE ONE THAT'S SHINING
ON YOUR FRIENDS BACK HOME.
THAT'S WHEN YOU'RE GRATEFUL
FOR ALL THOSE CLOCKS, COUNTING
OFF HOURS THAT ARE EXACTLY AS
LONG AT SEA AS THEY ARE ON
DRY LAND.

MASTERS AND SLAVES.

THE SHIP'S CAPTAIN IS OFFICIALLY
CALLED THE MASTER, A TITLE
I ASSOCIATE MORE WITH OLD
SOUTHERN SLAVE PLANTATIONS THAN
WITH FREIGHT SHIPS. STRICTLY
SPEAKING, IT'S NOT EVEN VERY
ACCURATE. THE REAL MASTERS
ARE THE GIANT TRANSNATIONAL
CORPORATIONS THAT OWN THESE
SHIPS, AND THAT CONTRACT
EMPLOYMENT AGENCIES IN PLACES
LIKE INDIA AND THE PHILIPPINES
TO HIRE THE CREW. IT'S NOT A
HAPPY ARRANGEMENT. THE SHIP
OWNERS ONLY CARE ABOUT THE
CARGO, AND THEY'RE ALWAYS
PRESSURING THE EMPLOYMENT
AGENCIES TO PRESSURE THE
CAPTAIN TO PRESSURE THE CREW
TO SPEED THINGS UP AND KEEP
COSTS DOWN. SO YEAH, THE CAPTAIN
IS THE MASTER OF THE SHIP, BUT

HE'S ALSO JUST A WAGE SLAVE.

AFTER A FEW DAYS AT SEA, I FIND
OUT THAT MOST OF THE SAILORS
ON BOARD HAVE BEEN ALL OVER
THE WORLD: NEW YORK, SHANGHAI,
SYDNEY, ISTANBUL. BUT BECAUSE
CONTAINERIZED FREIGHT CAN BE
LOADED AND UNLOADED SO QUICKLY,
THE SAILORS DON'T USUALLY HAVE
TIME TO GO ASHORE AND GET
BLIND DRUNK AND GET IN BRAWLS
THAT RESULT IN COLORFUL
SCARS OR THE NEED FOR A BLACK
EYEPATCH. FOR SIX MONTHS AT
A TIME, THE SAILORS CRUISE
FROM ONE CONTINENT TO THE
NEXT, AND THE ONLY THING
THAT CHANGES IS THE WEATHER.
COMPUTERS AND CRANES TAKE
CARE OF THE CARGO CONTAINERS,
SHUFFLING AND RESHUFFLING
THEM ACCORDING TO THE

MYSTERIOUS LOGIC OF GLOBAL
TRADE AND GLOBAL CAPITAL.
WHILE UP IN SPACE, SATELLITES
KEEP TRACK OF THE SHIP AND
THE SEA, AND BEAM DOWN
ORDERS FROM THE HOME OFFICE.
MAYBE ONE DAY, ONLY ROBOTS
WILL ROAM THE SEVEN SEAS,
CONTROLLED BY A SOFTWARE
PROGRAM CALLED MAGELLAN PRO,
OR COLUMBUS XL. AND
SAILING A FREIGHT SHIP WILL
BE ANOTHER JOB YOU CAN
TELECOMMUTE TO.

DAY SEVEN.

THE OFFICERS IN THE MESS EAT
THEIR MEALS IN SILENCE. MAYBE
THAT'S WHAT HAPPENS WHEN YOU
LIVE IN CLOSE QUARTERS WITH
THE SAME PEOPLE FOR MONTHS AT
A TIME. YOU PACE YOURSELF,
SPREADING YOUR CONVERSATIONS
ACROSS MANY MEALS. LENGTHENING
THE PAUSES BETWEEN WORDS
AND THE SILENCES BETWEEN
STORIES. ON A LONG VOYAGE,
CONVERSATION IS TOO PRECIOUS TO
GO WASTING ON SMALL TALK;
PRECIOUS THE WAY DRINKING
WATER USED TO BE BEFORE THE
INVENTION OF SALTWATER
DISTILLATION MACHINES.

I SPEND DAY SEVEN ON THE BRIDGE.
THE CHARTS SAY WE'RE GETTING
CLOSE TO THE SOUTHWEST TIP

OF IRELAND, AND I'M ANXIOUS TO CATCH SIGHT OF DRY LAND AFTER ALL THESE DAYS OF WATER AND SKY. I SUDDENLY REALIZE THAT NO COUNTRY I GO TO WILL BE HALF AS FOREIGN AS THE WET, WAVY ONE I JUST SPENT SEVEN DAYS IN. THE CAPTAIN MAKES A COUPLE CUPS OF HIS STRONG TEA AND TELLS ME THAT SAILING INTO LIVERPOOL IS TRICKY. FIRST, WE HAVE TO WAIT FOR HIGH TIDE, BECAUSE THE HARBOR'S NOT DEEP ENOUGH WHEN THE TIDE IS LOW. THEN THERE'S A REALLY NARROW LOCK TO NAVIGATE THROUGH. "LIVERPOOL ISN'T EASY, " THE CAPTAIN SAYS. I THINK I HEAR SOME EXCITEMENT IN HIS VOICE. JUST A HINT. THE EXCITEMENT OF SOMEONE WITH SKILLS WHO'S ABOUT TO GET A CHANCE TO USE THEM. THE

CREEPY NAVIGATION OFFICER IS
HANGING OUT ON THE BRIDGE, TOO.
5 O'CLOCK SHADOW AND SWEATY
PALMS. LOOKING LIKE THE KIND
OF GUY WHO LOITERS NEAR
GRADE SCHOOL PLAYGROUNDS OR
LITTLE LEAGUE GAMES. I ASK
HIM WHY, WITH ALL THE OTHER
HIGH TECH GEAR ON THE BRIDGE,
THERE ISN'T A DOPPLER WEATHER
RADAR. I MEAN, EVERY TV
METEOROLOGIST IN WEST TEXAS
HAS ONE TO KEEP AN EYE OUT
FOR TORNADOES. A RADAR THAT
COLOR CODES THE WEATHER:
WHEN THE CLOUDS ARE GREEN,
YOU DON'T HAVE TO WORRY; WHEN
THEY TURN RED, YOU WORRY.
GROWING UP, I SPENT EVERY SPRING
WATCHING THE WEATHER RADAR
AS TORNADOES DROPPED OUT OF THE

SKY AROUND MY HOMETOWN. FEEL-
ING AFRAID, BUT FEELING SOME-
THING ELSE, TOO. A KIND OF
THRILL. RECOGNIZING IN THE
WEATHER SOMETHING INSIDE ME:
THE CRAZY CHAOS OF BEING
THIRTEEN-YEARS-OLD, AND WINTER'S
OVER, AND IT'S SPRING. THE CREEPY
NAVIGATION OFFICER SEEMS
OFFENDED BY MY QUESTION. HE
TELLS ME THE SHIP GETS REGULAR
WEATHER UPDATES OVER THE
FAX MACHINE. "WE GET THE SAME
INFORMATION AIRPLANES GET.
AIRPLANES FLY IN THE AIR. WE
SAIL IN THE OCEAN. THIS IS THE
ONLY DIFFERENCE."

FOR THE REST OF THE AFTERNOON,
I STARE OUT THE WINDOW. STILL
NO IRELAND. FINALLY, AS THE
SUN'S GOING DOWN, THE VHF

CRACKLES TO LIFE. A VOICE
WITH A GAELIC ACCENT CALLS
OUT "ALL SHIPS, ALL SHIPS,
ALL SHIPS!" IT'S AN IRISH
COAST GUARD ADVISORY. I
STILL CAN'T SEE ANY LAND ON
THE HORIZON, BUT AFTER
SEVEN DAYS OF BOBBING IN
THE LIQUID CENTER OF THE
WORLD, AFTER SEVEN DAYS
AFLOAT, THIS VOICE ON THE
RADIO IS PRACTICALLY THE
SAME THING.

LIVERPOOL TRAIN.

THE 13:35 FROM LIVERPOOL TO
LONDON IS A VIRGIN TRAIN. THE
SAME VIRGIN THAT OWNS THE
RECORD COMPANY AND THE AIR-
LINE. A FEW YEARS BACK,
ENGLAND PRIVATIZED ITS RAIL
SYSTEM. IT PROBABLY WASN'T A
BAD IDEA, CONSIDERING HOW
MANY TIMES BRITISH RAIL TRAINS
KEPT FLYING OFF THE TRACKS.
BUT NOW THE TRAINS ARE LIKE
AIRPLANES, WHICH MEANS THEY'RE
CRAMMED FULL OF SEATS. THEY
SURE ARE SMOOTH, THOUGH. RAIL-
ROAD TRACKS IN EUROPE ARE
WELDED TOGETHER, NOT JOINTED
LIKE THEY ARE IN THE U.S. SO
THERE'S NO CLACKITY-CLACK ON
THIS TRAIN, JUST A DEEP, EVEN
RUMBLE, LIKE THE SOUND OF AN

ORCHESTRA DOING A ROLL ON THE TYMPANIS. IT'S A SOUND THAT MAKES EVERY MILE SEEM PORTENTOUS, THE PRELUDE TO SOME HUGE CLIMAX MARKED BY TRUMPETS AND MAYBE EVEN SOME CANON FIRE. INSTEAD, THE TRAIN ROLLS TO A STOP IN LONDON AND THE AIRBRAKES SIGH. MY PLAN IS TO GET OUT OF ENGLAND AS FAST AS I CAN. NOT BECAUSE I DON'T LIKE IT, BUT BECAUSE I CAN'T AFFORD IT. I WISH I COULD SPEND MORE TIME HERE, IN THE HOMELAND OF JOHN LOCKE, THOMAS PAINE, AND THE BUZZCOCKS; A LITTLE COUNTRY THAT'S RESPONSIBLE FOR SO MUCH THAT'S GOOD AND BAD ABOUT THE BIG COUNTRY I'M FROM. PLUS, IT'S NERDY. NOT ONE OF THOSE TOO-COOL-FOR-SCHOOL COUNTRIES

LIKE FRANCE OR ITALY. VISITING
ENGLAND IS LIKE GOING TO A
FAMILY REUNION AND DISCOVERING
THAT ALL YOUR DISTANT RELATIVES
ARE SORT OF AN EMBARRASSMENT.
ECCENTRIC REDNECKS WITH GOOD
GRAMMAR AND BAD TEETH.

IT'S A LOT CHEAPER TO TAKE A
FERRY TO FRANCE THAN TO RIDE
THE TRAIN THAT GOES THROUGH
THE CHUNNEL. BESIDES, I PREFER
TO BE ON TOP OF THE OCEAN RATHER
THAN UNDERNEATH IT. AT THE
FERRY TERMINAL IN DOVER, I
DISCOVER THERE ARE THREE
FERRY LINES TO CHOOSE FROM:
SEAFRANCE, NORFOLK, AND P&O.
I CHOOSE P&O BECAUSE I LIKE
ITS LOGO. IT LOOKS SORT OF
LIKE THIS:

BLUE →   ← WHITE
         ← RED
↳ YELLOW

N THE OUTSIDE, THE FERRY LOOKS
LIKE A FERRY, BUT INSIDE, IT
LOOKS LIKE THE FOOD COURT AT
THE MALL. THERE ARE A HALF-
DOZEN RESTAURANTS AND
CAFES ON THE VARIOUS DECKS.
I WALK ALL OVER THE SHIP
LOOKING FOR A PLACE TO SIT,
TILL I FINALLY FIGURE OUT
THAT THE ONLY PLACE TO SIT IS
AT A TABLE IN ONE OF THESE
RESTAURANTS. I CHOOSE A PLACE
CALLED THE HORIZON LOUNGE.
SITTING THERE WITH MY BIG
BACKPACK PLUNKED DOWN NEXT
TO ME, SURROUNDED BY DAY-
TRIPPING ENGLISH FAMILIES, I
FEEL CONSPICUOUS. LIKE A
HOMELESS GUY WHO'S WANDERED
INTO A T.G.I. FRIDAY'S.
IN CALAIS, MY HIGH SCHOOL FRENCH
STARTS TO COME BACK TO ME.

"IL PLEUT," I SAY AS IT STARTS TO POUR. "IL FAIT FROID," I SAY AS I START TO SHIVER. I FIND A HOSTEL, A BIG, MODERN PLACE. THE GUY AT THE RECEPTION DESK SITS IN FRONT OF FOUR SURVEILLANCE MONITORS WITH PICTURES OF FOUR EMPTY HALLWAYS. MY ROOM HAS TWO BEDS. THERE'S A SMALL SUITCASE ON ONE OF THE BEDS WITH A CAREFULLY FOLDED STRIPED TOWEL LYING ON TOP. THE OWNER OF THE STRIPED TOWEL NEVER APPEARS.

IN THE MORNING, I GET BREAKFAST DOWNSTAIRS. THE BREAKFAST ROOM IS HUGE, WITH DOZENS OF LONG TABLES. I'M THE ONLY ONE IN THERE, EXCEPT FOR A GUY SITTING IN THE CORNER WITH HIS BACK TOWARD ME. I GRAB

A CUP OF COFFEE AND A BOWL OF
CORNFLAKES FROM THE BUFFET
AND FEEL LIKE I'M BEING WATCHED.
MAYBE BY THE GUY AT THE
RECEPTION DESK, WATCHING ME
ON ONE OF HIS TV MONITORS.
ZOOMING IN ON MY COFFEE CUP.
TAKING CAREFUL NOTES IN A
NEAT HAND. I SIT DOWN AND
START TO EAT MY CEREAL. THE
SOUND OF MY CRUNCHING CAUSES
THE GUY IN THE CORNER TO
TURN AROUND. HE GIVES ME AN
ANNOYED LOOK.

LATER ON, I CATCH A TRAIN TO
LILLES. IT'S A LOCAL TRAIN
WITH GRAFFITI SPRAYPAINTED ON
ALL THE WINDOWS. I BOARD THE
TRAIN BEHIND A GUY AND HIS
DAUGHTER. SHE'S MAYBE 8-YEARS-
OLD. THE DAD KISSES THE KID
GOODBYE, AND HE ASKS THE

CONDUCTOR TO LOOK OUT FOR HER.
THE CONDUCTOR NODS AND SMILES.
THE LITTLE GIRL HAS A BLACK,
KID-SIZED VALISE AND A SERIOUS
EXPRESSION. FOR THE NEXT
FEW STOPS, I FEEL LIKE I'VE
STUMBLED INTO SOME DREAMED-
UP WORLD. A PLACE BEYOND
HARM, WHERE SCHOOL KIDS RIDE
ALONE ON THE LOCAL TRAINS
PAST COUNTRY HOUSES WITH
RED TILE ROOFS. AT A VILLAGE
CALLED AUDRUICQ, THE LITTLE
GIRL STEPS OFF. THEN THE
TRAIN ROLLS BACK INTO THE
WORLD I'M FROM, WHERE
THERE'S NO SUCH THING AS A
PLACE BEYOND HARM.

Roken in de Trein

THE TRAIN STATION IN LILLES HAS
A VAULTED CEILING SET WITH
A MILLION PANES OF GLASS. THE
GLASS IS TINTED PINK, WHICH
MAKES THE STATION LOOK LIKE
SOMETHING YOU'D HALLUCINATE
AFTER SOMEONE SLIPPED A
DESIGNER DRUG INTO YOUR ENERGY
DRINK AT A DANCE CLUB IN
AMSTERDAM. COPS WEARING
PINK-TINTED CAMO WALK PAST
WITH PINK-TINTED SUBMACHINE
GUNS. A PINKISH BOMB-SNIFFING
DOG SNIFFS MY PINKISH BACK-
PACK.

I HOP ON A TRAIN HEADING TO
ANTWERP. I KNOW WE'VE CROSSED
FROM FRANCE TO BELGIUM
WHEN THE TRAIN STATIONS START
TO HAVE NAMES WITH DOUBLE-

VOWELS OR J'S FOLLOWED BY A CONSONANT. THE ELECTRONIC MESSAGE BOARD AT THE FRONT OF THE TRAIN SAYS STUFF LIKE "WE KOMEN AAN IN GENT-SINT-PIETERS," AND "ROKEN IN DE TREIN? NEEN DANK U." I BEGIN TO SUSPECT THAT FLEMISH IS AN IMAGINARY LANGUAGE INVENTED BY THE SCI-FI/FANTASY CLUB AT SOME AMERICAN HIGH SCHOOL DURING LUNCH PERIOD. IN FACT, I BEGIN TO SUSPECT THAT THE ENTIRE POPULATION OF BELGIUM MAY BE DESCENDED FROM A HIGH SCHOOL SCI-FI/FANTASY CLUB. IN FRANCE, PEOPLE WEAR COOL SPIKY HAIRDOS AND DESIGNER EYEWEAR. IN BELGIUM, THEY WEAR FANNY PACKS.

IN ANTWERP, I CATCH A TRAIN TO ROTTERDAM, AND NEXT THING I KNOW, I'M SITTING ON THE COUCH IN BECKY AND ROSIE'S PLACE. BECKY AND ROSIE ARE TWO VERY COOL ARTISTS I KNOW FROM CHICAGO. EVEN THOUGH THEY'RE LIVING AND WORKING IN HOLLAND ILLEGALLY, THEY SOMEHOW SCAMMED A GOVERNMENT-SUBSIDIZED APARTMENT. THEY TELL ME HOLLAND IS LIKE THAT. THEY ALSO TELL ME THAT, AS AMERICANS, IT MAKES THEM A LITTLE SUSPICIOUS. "HOW CAN YOU BE PUNK ROCK WHEN THE MAYOR IS PAYING YOUR RENT?" BECKY WANTS TO KNOW. AFTER A DAY OR TWO, I GET A BIG CRUSH ON ROTTERDAM. IT'S LIKE CHICAGO IN THE YEAR 3000 AD, WHEN THAT CITY HAS WORKED OUT

ALL ITS KINKS. THERE'S AN ELEVATED TRAIN, BUT IT'S SLEEK AND SILENT AND HIGH-TECH, AND THERE ARE BIKE LANES, BUT THERE ARE ALSO BIKE TRAFFIC LIGHTS AND A BIKE TUNNEL THAT RUNS UNDER THE MAAS RIVER. IT'S A CITY WHERE YOU CAN WALK DOWN THE STREET SMOKING A FAT DOOBIE, AND WHERE THE HOOKERS HAVE THEIR OWN CITY-FINANCED COMPOUND THAT LOOKS A LITTLE LIKE A SONIC DRIVE-IN, EXCEPT THE WAITRESSES DON'T BRING YOU BURGERS AND MILKSHAKES BUT, INSTEAD, THEY GET IN THE CAR WITH YOU.

BECKY AND ROSIE TAKE ME TO A TURKISH BAR. IT'S 3 IN THE MORNING, AND THE PLACE IS FULL OF OLDER TURKISH GUYS. EVERYONE IS WEARING SUITS AND FLASHY WATCHES.

"IS THIS PLACE OKAY?" I WHISPER TO BECKY. SHE SMILES AND SHRUGS. WE SPEND THE NEXT COUPLE HOURS DRINKING BOTTLES OF HEINEKIN THAT VARIOUS GUYS IN THE BAR KEEP BUYING FOR US. IT TURNS OUT THAT HEINEKIN TASTES EXACTLY THE SAME IN THE COUNTRY IT'S FROM AS IT DOES ANYWHERE ELSE. IT'S SORT OF A RELIEF: REALIZING THAT YOU DON'T ACTUALLY HAVE TO GO ALL THE WAY TO HOLLAND TO GET A GOOD HEINEKIN, BECAUSE IT DOESN'T TASTE ALL THAT GREAT HERE, EITHER. IT'S A RELIEF BECAUSE IT MEANS THAT JUST BECAUSE YOU'RE STUCK IN A LITTLE TOWN IN TEXAS, OR ON A LITTLE PLANET IN A BACKWATER SOLAR SYSTEM,

DOESN'T NECESSARILY MEAN YOU'RE
MISSING OUT ON MUCH.

ROSIE AND BECKY FILL ME IN ON
THE DUTCH LIFE. DUTCH BOYS,
THEY TELL ME, ARE HARD TO
DATE. THEY'RE QUIET AND THEY
NEVER MAKE THE FIRST MOVE.
DUTCH GIRLS, ON THE OTHER
HAND, ARE TOF - TOUGH - AND
CALL ALL THE SHOTS. THEY
TELL ME THAT THE NETHERLANDS
IS PRETTY GREAT, BUT IT'S
HAVING AN IDENTITY CRISIS
RIGHT NOW. FOR YEARS, IT
WAS A COUNTRY THAT WELCOMED
IMMIGRANTS AND PRIDED IT-
SELF ON ITS TOLERANCE.
"LIVING TOGETHER SEPARATELY"_
THAT WAS THE POLICY. BUT
NOW THE DUTCH ARE HAVING
SECOND THOUGHTS ABOUT
IMMIGRATION, ESPECIALLY
MOROCCAN IMMIGRANTS WITH

CONSERVATIVE ISLAMIC VALUES. THE ASSASSINATION OF PIM FORTUYN, A POPULAR ANTI-IMMIGRATION POLITICIAN, AND THE MURDER OF THEO VAN GOGH, A FILMMAKER WHO WAS CRITICAL OF ISLAMIC FUNDAMENTALISM (AND WHO WAS KILLED WHILE RIDING HIS BIKE IN AMSTERDAM BY AN OUTRAGED DUTCH-MOROCCAN GUY) HAVE ONLY MADE THINGS WORSE. THE FUNNY THING, IF YOU CAN SAY THERE'S ANYTHING FUNNY ABOUT ALL THIS, IS THAT IT'S ONLY IN A PLACE LIKE HOLLAND THAT YOU CAN BE KIND OF SYMPATHETIC TO THE ANTI-IMMIGRATION CROWD. SURE, THERE ARE ASSHOLE RACISTS AMONG THEM, BUT FOR A LOT OF THE DUTCH, THEIR ONLY BEEF WITH THE MUSLIM IMMIGRANTS IS THAT THEY'RE NOT LIBERAL ENOUGH. AND MAYBE THEY HAVE

A POINT. I MEAN, IT SEEMS LIKE
THE WORLD WOULD BE A BETTER
PLACE IF MORE OF US WERE
LIKE THE DUTCH.

ALL THIS TALK OF HOLLAND
GETTING LESS TOLERANT BUMS
ME OUT. I MEAN, THIS IS THE
COUNTRY I ALWAYS IMAGINE
FLEEING TO WHEN THE RIGHT-
WING MILITIAS AND THE
RELIGIOUS FANATICS AND THE
SECRET POLICE FINALLY TAKE
OVER AMERICA. I ALWAYS
THOUGHT I COULD JUST MOVE TO
ROTTERDAM AND FALL IN LOVE
WITH A TOF DUTCH GIRL AND
RIDE MY BIKE HAPPILY INTO
THE SUNSET. I GUESS I SHOULD
HAVE KNOWN BETTER.

BERLIN TRAIN.

THE BERLIN TRAIN PULLS CONFI-
DENTLY OUT OF ROTTERDAM'S
CENTRAL STATION AND SPEEDS
FORWARD WITH A KIND OF
ASSURANCE I CAN ONLY DREAM
OF HAVING. ME AND MY HESITANT
FORWARD MOTION. ALWAYS
SHUFFLING AND SECOND-GUESSING.
EARLY THIS MORNING, I SAID SO
LONG TO ROSIE AND BECKY AND
I GOT ON THE SUBWAY. AT ONE
STOP, AS THIS CUTE DUTCH GIRL
WAS ABOUT TO GET OFF THE TRAIN,
AN OLDER LADY STOPPED HER AND
POINTED OUT THAT HER PURSE WAS
UNFASTENED. THE OLDER LADY
SAID SOMETHING IN DUTCH —
"YOU CAN NEVER BE TOO CAREFUL,"
MAYBE — AND THE CUTE GIRL
SMILED AND SAID THANKS. I
SMILED, TOO, AT THIS ONE
LITTLE MOMENT OF CIVILITY

THAT THIS CIVIL LITTLE COUNTRY IS MADE OUT OF. A COUNTRY WHERE EVERYONE IS TALL, AND THE TRAINS ARE PAINTED MUSTARD-YELLOW, AND HALF THE PLACE HAS BEEN RECOVERED FROM THE SEA.

A COUPLE NIGHTS AGO, I MET A GUY FROM SAN FRANCISCO WHO'S BEEN LIVING IN ROTTERDAM FOR THE LAST FEW YEARS. HE TELLS ME THERE AREN'T SO MANY UPS AND DOWNS IN HOLLAND, COMPARED TO THE U.S. IT'S MOSTLY SMOOTH SAILING, WHICH CAN BE NICE, BUT WHICH CAN MAKE YOU A LITTLE RESTLESS, TOO. HE LIKES HOLLAND, BUT HE CAN'T STAY HERE. HE'S A CALIFORNIAN. HE SAYS HE MISSES THE DESERT. THE ENDLESS EMPTINESS OF IT.

I LEAVE ROTTERDAM WITH A
SMOKER'S COUGH, EVEN THOUGH I
DON'T SMOKE. MINERS IN WEST
VIRGINIA GET BLACK LUNG FROM
WORKING IN THE COAL MINES,
AND VISITORS TO ROTTERDAM
GET IT FROM SPENDING TOO MUCH
TIME IN SMOKY BARS. SMOKER'S
COUGH IS JUST A SYMPTOM OF
WHAT THE DUTCH CALL GEZELLIGHEID-
BEING SOCIABLE. DUTCH PEOPLE
PUT A PREMIUM ON GEZELLIGHEID.
AT NIGHT, EVERYONE GOES OUT
TOGETHER FOR A DRINK, AND IN THE
MORNING, EVERYONE'S GOT A
SMOKER'S COUGH. I'M NOT SURE,
BUT I THINK GEZELLIGHEID HAS
SOMETHING TO DO WITH LIVING IN
A COUNTRY THAT THE SEA IS
ALWAYS THREATENING TO SWALLOW
UP. IN A COUNTRY LIKE THAT,
YOU HAVE TO GET ALONG WITH

EACH OTHER. YOU HAVE TO DRINK
TOGETHER AND BUILD DIKES
TOGETHER. OTHERWISE, YOU'RE SUNK.

ON THE WAY HOME FROM THE
BAR, I RIDE ON THE BACK OF
ROSIE'S BIKE, DUTCH STYLE:
SITTING SIDE-SADDLE ON THE
LITTLE RACK ABOVE THE BACK
WHEEL. EVERY DUTCH BIKE HAS
A LITTLE RACK LIKE THAT.
ANOTHER OPPORTUNITY FOR
GEZELLIGHEID. THE TRICK IS TO
LET THE BIKE RIDER GET A HEAD
START. THEN YOU RUN UP FROM
BEHIND AND GRAB THE RIDER
AROUND THE WAIST AND HOP
ABOARD. THE BIKE WOBBLES FOR
A SECOND, A LITTLE UNSTEADY.
A LITTLE UNCERTAIN. THEN
EVERYTHING STRAIGHTENS OUT
AND YOU RIDE ALONG BEHIND

YOUR PAL, BREATHING IN THE
SMOKY SMELL OF HER JACKET.
ROLLING PAST THE SCIENCE -
FICTION SKYSCRAPERS AND THE
DARK STOREFRONTS, AND IGNORING
ALL THE BICYCLE TRAFFIC LIGHTS.
RIDING DUTCH-STYLE GIVES YOU
AN EXCUSE TO HOLD YOUR FRIEND
TIGHT AS SHE HAULS YOU UP ONE
SIDE OF THE BIG WHITE ERASMUS
BRIDGE, AND AS YOU SPEED A
LITTLE OUT OF CONTROL DOWN
THE OTHER SIDE.

CALAIS, FRANCE

ESSEN.

MY PAL SERGIO IS AN ITALIAN GUY
WHO LIVES WITH HIS GERMAN
GIRLFRIEND ANYA IN ESSEN.
BEHIND THEIR APARTMENT, THERE'S
A COURTYARD. ON A SUNNY
SATURDAY IN THE MIDDLE OF APRIL,
IT'S PARADISE BACK THERE:
GREEN GRASS SPECKED WITH
WHITE CLOVERS, AND FLOWER
POTS ON ALL THE WINDOW SILLS.
ON A DAY LIKE TODAY, IT'S
IMPOSSIBLE TO FIGURE OUT WHAT
WENT WRONG SEVEN DECADES AGO,
WHEN THIS COUNTRY LOST ITS
MIND. THIS COUNTRY IN PAR-
TICULAR, WITH ITS CLIPPED
HEDGES AND ITS LACE CURTAINS.
GOOD BEER AND APPLE STRUEDEL.
A PLACE WHERE THE TRAINS
REALLY DO RUN ON TIME, AND
PEOPLE CAREFULLY SORT THEIR

RECYCLABLES. ITS ALWAYS TEMPT-
ING TO PSYCHOANALYZE
GERMANY; TO MAKE A CONNECTION
BETWEEN CAREFULLY SORTED
RECYCLABLES AND FASCIST
POLITICS. IT'S TEMPTING, BUT
IT'S PROBABLY NOT FAIR.
ANYHOW, THIS PERFECT COURTYARD
BEHIND SERGIO AND ANYA'S
APARTMENT MAKES ME A LITTLE
SAD. MAYBE BECAUSE IT'S IN A
COUNTRY WITH SUCH A CRUMMY
HISTORY. OR MAYBE BECAUSE
EVERY COURTYARD IN THE WORLD
IS A LITTLE SAD WHEN IT'S
SPRING, AND THE SUN IS OUT AND
THE BREEZE IS WARM. SERGIO
SAYS IT'S JUST BIOLOGY. A GENETIC
RESPONSE TO THE SPRINGTIME.
OUR BODY'S WAY OF LETTING US
KNOW THAT WHAT WE OUGHT TO
BE DOING IS FALLING IN LOVE AND
FINDING SOME GRASSY MEADOW
TO DO IT IN. 171

SERGIO MAKES PASTA FOR DINNER.
HE TAKES PASTA VERY SERIOUSLY.
HE MAKES THE SAUCE FROM SCRATCH.
ZUCCHINIS AND TOMATOES AND A
SPECIAL KIND OF MOZZARELLA
CHEESE THAT JUST BARELY MEETS
HIS STANDARDS. "GERMANS KNOW
NOTHING ABOUT MOZZARELLA
CHEESE," HE INFORMS ME.

IN THE MORNING, ANYA MAKES
PANCAKES FROM A RECIPE SHE
FINDS IN HER "AMERIKA
KOCHBUCH." THE PANCAKES ARE
WAY BETTER THAN ANY I'VE EVER
HAD IN AMERIKA. ANYA FLIPS
THROUGH HER COOKBOOK AND ASKS
ME IF I'VE EVER HEARD OF A DISH
CALLED "CLAM CHOWDER." I TELL
HER IT'S PRONOUNCED "CLAM
CHOW-DAH" AND PEOPLE EAT IT
IN BOSTON. I ALSO TELL HER WHAT
MAPLE SYRUP IS, AND WHERE NEW

MEXICO IS LOCATED, AND HOW TO PRONOUNCE THE WORD "SCISSORS." SERGIO IS AN ITALIAN WHO DOESN'T SPEAK GERMAN, AND ANYA IS A GERMAN WHO DOESN'T SPEAK ITALIAN, SO THE TWO OF THEM SPEAK TO EACH OTHER IN ENGLISH. NOW AND THEN, ANYA OR SERGIO WILL STOP IN MID-SENTENCE, TRYING TO THINK OF AN ENGLISH WORD. THEN THEY'LL HELP EACH OTHER OUT, SUGGESTING POSSIBILITIES. WHEN THEY FINALLY FIGURE OUT THE RIGHT WORD, IT'S A SMALL VICTORY. IT MAKES ME THINK THIS SHOULD BE ADDED TO THE LIST OF "TIPS TO IMPROVE YOUR SEX LIFE" THAT YOU FIND IN THOSE GLOSSY MAGA-ZINES AT THE CHECK-OUT COUNTER. TIP NO. 16: SPEAK TO EACH OTHER IN A FOREIGN LANGUAGE.

IN THE AFTERNOON, SERGIO TAKES ME
FOR A DRIVE AROUND THE
RUHRGEBIET — LITERALLY, THE
"RUHR REGION," BECAUSE THE RUHR
RIVER RUNS THROUGH THIS PART OF
GERMANY. IT WAS ONCE ONE OF
THE GREAT INDUSTRIAL CENTERS OF
THE PLANET, THE PITTSBURGH OF
GERMANY, FULL OF GIANT FIRE-
BREATHING FACTORIES. THE REGION
IS MOSTLY A FLAT PLAIN, EXCEPT
FOR A FEW ENORMOUS SLAG
HEAPS LEFT BEHIND FROM THE
COAL MINES. ON TOP OF ONE OF
THESE MAN-MADE MOUNTAINS, A
GUY NAMED WOLFGANG CHRIST
BUILT THE TETRAHEDRON. IT'S A
SCI-FI OBSERVATION PLATFORM
BUILT OUT OF STEEL PIPES.
PICTURE A PYRAMID-SHAPED
JUNGLE-GYM THAT'S BEEN

ZAPPED BY A MARTIAN GROWTH RAY. AFTER YOU CLIMB A FEW THOUSAND STEPS TO THE TOP OF THE THING, YOU CAN LOOK OUT OVER THE RUHRGEBIET: A MILLION ACRES OF PALE GREEN PIERCED HERE AND THERE BY SKYSCRAPING SMOKESTACKS. UP TOP, SERGIO TELLS ME HE LIKES GERMANS, BUT HE WORRIES ABOUT THEM, TOO. IN ITALY, NO ONE OBEYS THE RULES, ESPECIALLY IF THE RULES ARE STUPID. BUT GERMANS TEND TO OBEY THE RULES NO MATTER WHAT. IT MAY BE THEIR FATAL FLAW, HE TELLS ME. I GIVE SERGIO MY OWN TAKE ON GERMANS: THAT IF GERMANY WERE A PERSON, HE'D BE THE GUY WHO READS THE TECH MANUAL FOR HIS VCR FROM COVER TO COVER.

SERGIO NODS. "THAT'S WHY EVERY GERMAN GIRL SHOULD HAVE AN ITALIAN BOYFRIEND," HE SAYS. WE STAND ON THE TETRAHEDRON TILL THE SUN SETS. THEN WE MAKE OUR WAY BACK TO SERGIO'S CAR IN THE DARK. I ASK SERGIO WHAT THE GERMAN WORD FOR FLASHLIGHT IS. BLITZLICHT, HE TELLS ME. A WORD THAT, LIKE A LOT OF STUFF IN THIS COUNTRY, MANAGES TO BE BOTH GOOFY AND A LITTLE SINISTER AT THE SAME TIME.

EURO-NIGHT

I TAKE THE OVERNIGHT TRAIN TO
VIENNA: A EURO-NIGHT TRAIN
THAT LOOKS LIKE IT ROLLED
INTO THE STATION DIRECT FROM
1975. THE SEATS ARE COVERED
WITH OLD ORANGE AND BROWN
UPHOLSTERY, AND IN FACT THE
WHOLE TRAIN LOOKS LIKE IT WAS
FURNISHED BY A DUMPSTER DIVER.
THE SEATS LOOK SLEPT ON,
SAGGED AND STAINED, LUMPY.
LIKE THEY'VE TAKEN ON THE
CONTOURS OF ALL THOSE RESTLESS
NIGHTS, AND OF THE KIND OF
SLEEP YOU SLEEP ON TRAINS.
AS WE GET NEAR VIENNA, MY
COMPARTMENT FILLS UP WITH
MORNING COMMUTERS. FRESHLY
SHOWERED PEOPLE IN OFFICE
CLOTHES WHO LOOK AT ME WITH

PITY, OR MAYBE DISGUST, THIS
STUBBLY, CRUMPLED GUY SLOUCHED
IN THE SEAT IN FRONT OF THEM.

I ARRIVE IN VIENNA WITHOUT
A MAP OR A GUIDE BOOK AND GO
LOOKING FOR A CUP OF COFFEE.
I CAN'T FIND ONE. THIS IS
PROBABLY THE WORLD'S CAPITAL
OF COFFEE DRINKING, BUT SOME-
HOW, I CAN'T FIND ONE LOUSY
CUP OF THE STUFF. IT SEEMS
CRUEL, LIKE DYING OF THIRST
NEXT TO NIAGARA FALLS. I
FINALLY FIND A PLACE, A LITTLE
COFFEE SHOP ON A SIDE STREET.
SOMEONE'S SCRAWLED "FUCK
NIGGER" ON A WALL BY THE
DOOR.

VIENNA LOOKS LIKE A TOWN
DESIGNED BY SOMEONE WITH A
DEGREE IN MORTUARY SCIENCE.

IT'S OPULENT THE WAY A CRYPT
IS: ALL CARVED MARBLE AND
GILDING AND JUNKIE ANGELS
GIVING YOU DIRTY LOOKS FROM
THE ROOFTOPS. WHEN THE SKY
HANGS LOW AND GRAY, IT'S LIKE
YOU'RE WANDERING THROUGH A
CEMETERY INSTEAD OF A CITY.
MAYBE THAT EXPLAINS ALL THE
COFFEE-DRINKING THAT GOES ON
IN THIS TOWN. IN SEATTLE, YOU
DRINK COFFEE BECAUSE OF THE
RAIN. IN VIENNA, YOU DRINK IT
BECAUSE OF THE MARBLE.
LATER, I WIND UP AT A PLACE
CALLED THE CAFÉ HUMMEL, A
PROPER VIENNESE COFFEE HOUSE
WHERE THE WAITER WEARS A
TUXEDO AND HE'S AN ASSHOLE
AND HE SHORTCHANGES ME WHEN
I PAY THE BILL. I ORDER A
BRAUNER, WHICH IS SORT OF AN

AUSTRIAN CAPPUCCINO. IT'S GOOD.
REALLY GOOD. THEN I FLOAT OUT
OF THE CAFÉ HUMMEL ON A
CAFFEINE CLOUD, SMILING AT THE
SKINHEADS AND THE GRAY SKIES.
CERTAIN, ALL THE SUDDEN, THAT
VIENNA IS THE MOST ELEGANT
CITY IN THE WORLD.

VIENNA

HITLER WAS A VEGETARIAN

VIENNA IS AN EASY TOWN TO FIND A
VEGETARIAN RESTAURANT IN. IT'S
SURPRISING. I MEAN, IT'S NOT
EXACTLY A HIPPY TOWN. I DECIDE
I SHOULD JUST BE GRATEFUL AND
NOT THINK TOO DEEPLY ABOUT
WHAT IT ALL MEANS, OR
WHY HITLER WAS A VEGETARIAN.
THERE'S A PARTICULARLY GOOD
RESTAURANT ON THE JUDENPLATZ,
NEAR THE MONUMENT TO THE
65,000 AUSTRIAN JEWS WHO WERE
MURDERED DURING THE HOLOCAUST.
THE MONUMENT IS A SQUAT
CEMENT BOX, ABOUT THE SIZE OF
A 2-CAR GARAGE. THE WALLS
ARE MOLDED TO LOOK LIKE
LIBRARY SHELVES: HUNDREDS OF
CONCRETE BOOKS STACKED ON
CONCRETE SHELVES. I READ THAT
THESE CONCRETE BOOKS ARE A

LIBRARY OF UNTOLD STORIES: THE
STORIES OF THE SILENT DEAD.
I'M GLAD THE MEMORIAL IS THERE,
BUT AS I EAT A PLATE OF VEGGIE
WURSTS, I COME UP WITH MY OWN
PROPOSAL FOR AN AUSTRIAN
HOLOCAUST MEMORIAL: I'D DEFACE
ONE OVER-RESTORED, OVER-
MAINTAINED VIENNESE BUILDING
FOR EVERY JEW WHO WAS KILLED.
MAYBE A GASH ACROSS THE
FAÇADE, OR A BIG, RAGGED HOLE
IN THE WALL. A COUPLE DOZEN
PERMANENTLY SHATTERED WINDOWS.
THE OWNER OF THE BUILDING
COULD CHOOSE THE KIND OF DIS-
FIGUREMENT, SUBJECT TO THE
APPROVAL OF THE MONUMENT
COMMISSION. I DON'T MEAN TO
PUT DOWN THIS LITTLE MONUMENT
IN THE JUDENPLATZ, BUT IT SEEMS
LIKE ITS SCALE IS OFF. SHOULDN'T

THE MONUMENT BE AS BIG AS
VIENNA? MARKING THE WHOLE
CITY WITH ITS CRIME?

I GO BACK TO THE VEGGIE REST-
AURANT ON THE JUDENPLATZ A
COUPLE TIMES. I LIKE THE
PLACE BECAUSE YOU CAN GET
VEGETARIAN VERSIONS OF ALL
THOSE ÜBER-MEATY TEUTONIC
DISHES. STUFF LIKE HUGE GREASY
DUMPLINGS AND TURGID SAUSAGES
AND STEAMING PILES OF SAUER-
KRAUT THAT, IN THEIR ORIGINAL
FORMS, ARE A CRIME AGAINST
NATURE, BUT WHEN PREPARED
VEGAN-STYLE AND ACCOMPANIED
BY A BIG GLASS OF BEER ARE
REALLY DAMN TASTY. AFTER A
MEAL LIKE THAT, I FEEL BETTER
ABOUT THIS TOWN. I MEAN,
ISN'T A VEGAN VERSION OF SOME

MONSTROUS AUSTRIAN DISH
PRACTICALLY AN ACT OF
CONTRITION?
ONE NIGHT, WHILE I'M EATING AT
THE PLACE, THE VIENNA VEG-
ETARIAN SOCIETY CONVENES AT
THE TABLE NEXT TO MINE.
EVERY TIME A NEW PERSON
SHOWS UP AT THE TABLE, THERE'S
A ROUND OF PAINFULLY AWKWARD
INTRODUCTIONS. IT CHOKES ME
UP, ALL THESE PEOPLE WHO WERE
RAISED TO BE RESERVED AND A
LITTLE STANDOFFISH, TRYING
THEIR BEST TO BE FRIENDLY TO
EACH OTHER. TRYING HARD TO
GET PAST THE STIFFNESS THEY
WERE BORN INTO.

CHEESE FOR BREAKFAST

FORGIVE ME FOR STARING, JAPANESE
GIRLS AT THE NEXT TABLE. I
CAN'T HELP IT. THREE OF YOU,
STILL IN YOUR PAJAMAS, EATING
BROTCHENS WITH ORANGE MARM-
ALADE AND SIPPING TEA IN BARE
LEGS AND SANDALS. EVEN AT A
DUMPY HOTEL LIKE THIS ONE,
BREAKFAST COMES WITH THE ROOM.
I'M FROM A COUNTRY OF MOTEL 6'S,
WHERE THE ONLY THING YOU GET
IN THE MORNING IS A STYROFOAM
CUP OF BAD COFFEE THAT YOU
PLUNGER OUT OF A THERMOS IN
THE LOBBY. A COUNTRY OF MOTELS
WHERE YOU SLEEP LIGHTLY ON
THE MATTRESSES AND YOU BARELY
LEAVE A TRACE. JUST SOME
WRINKLED SHEETS AND A DAMP
TOWEL AND THE FAINT IMPRESSION
OF YOUR SIGNATURE ON A CREDIT

CARD SLIP PRESSED THROUGH
PURPLE CARBON PAPER. A FAINT
IMPRESSION OF YOUR PASSING,
FILED AWAY IN A DRAWER IN THE
LOBBY. EVEN IN A DUMPY HOTEL
IN VIENNA, YOU GET A FREE
BREAKFAST, THOUGH YOU MAY NOT
WANT IT: A COUPLE SLICES OF
CHEESE, A COUPLE SLICES OF
SOME PINK, VEINED MEAT. COFFEE
AND BREAD ROLLS. THE REAL
REASON TO GO TO BREAKFAST IS
TO SEE WHO ELSE IS STAYING AT
THE HOTEL. A RUSSIAN FAMILY,
IT TURNS OUT, AND THESE 3
JAPANESE GIRLS, AND ME. THE
JAPANESE GIRLS LAUGH AT THE
FOOD. "I WONDER WHAT'S FOR
BREAKFAST TOMORROW?" ONE
OF THEM SUDDENLY ASKS IN
ENGLISH. "CHEESE IS FOR

BREAKFAST, "ANOTHER ONE
ANSWERS. THEN THEY LAUGH
SOME MORE, SHATTERING THE
STILLNESS VIENNA SEEMS TO
HAVE NO SHORTAGE OF. I READ
SOMEWHERE THAT THE VIENNESE
LOVE THEIR BUILDINGS AND
THEIR DOGS, BUT DON'T PARTIC-
ULARLY LIKE EACH OTHER.
I READ SOMEWHERE ELSE THAT
AUSTRIA HAS ONE OF THE
HIGHEST SUICIDE RATES IN THE
WORLD. I WONDER IF THE
JAPANESE GIRLS KNOW THIS, AND
IF THEY THINK VIENNA IS AS
CREEPY AS I DO. THEY PROBABLY
JUST THINK I'M CREEPY, STARING
AT THEM WHILE THEY EAT
CHEESE FOR BREAKFAST.

CROATIA

WHEN I MEET TOMISLAV IN
BERLIN, SERGIO TELLS HIM I'M
BOTH A VEGETARIAN AND I
DON'T SMOKE. "WELL," HE SAYS,
BLOWING A CLOUD OF CIGARETTE
SMOKE IN MY FACE, "I GUESS
YOU'LL DIE HEALTHY." A COUPLE
WEEKS LATER, TOMISLAV
INVITES ME TO ZAGREB, WHERE
HE LIVES. HE TELLS ME I CAN
SHOW MY MOVIES AT THE LITTLE
THEATER WHERE HE WORKS.
I GO TO THE TRAIN STATION IN
VIENNA TO BUY A TICKET.
"ONE-WAY TO ZAGREB," I SAY,
FEELING BADASS. LIKE SOME
COLD WAR DOUBLE-AGENT
CROSSING THE IRON CURTAIN.
AT THE AUSTRIA-SLOVENIA
BORDER, THE TRAIN LURCHES TO
A STOP. A LADY CONDUCTOR

WITH DARK EYES COMES INTO MY
COMPARTMENT. "---" SHE SAYS.
I HAND HER MY TICKET. SHE
STAMPS IT. "-- ---, ---"
SHE SAYS. I SMILE. SHE SMILES.
AFTER AN AWKWARD MOMENT OR
TWO, SHE WALKS AWAY.

THE TRAIN STARTS ROLLING
AGAIN, THROUGH A COUNTRY OF
CRUMBLING BUILDINGS AND
FRESHLY PAVED HIGHWAYS. A
LANDSCAPE IN TRANSITION. IN
A COUPLE MONTHS, SLOVENIA
JOINS THE EUROPEAN UNION,
AND IT'S STILL STRUGGLING TO
MEET E.U. STANDARDS. AS THE
SUN SETS, WE ROLL INTO CROATIA,
WHERE THE BUILDINGS ARE
CRUMBLING AND THE HIGHWAYS
AREN'T FRESHLY PAVED. CROATIA

IS SUPPOSED TO JOIN THE E.U., TOO,
BUT SO FAR, NO ONE HAS SET
A FIRM DATE.

TOMISLAV RESERVED A ROOM FOR
ME AT THE HOTEL ASTORIA.
WHEN I GET TO ZAGREB, I FIND
THE PLACE AND CHECK IN. IT'S
A 3-STAR HOTEL. IN THE OLD
EASTERN BLOC, HOTELS ARE
GIVEN STARS FOR THE NUMBER OF
STAINS ON THE CARPET. A
5-STAR HOTEL IS REALLY SOME-
THING: A BAROQUE CATHEDRAL
OF STAINS. THE HOTEL ASTORIA
ISN'T WORLD-CLASS, BUT IT'S
RESPECTABLE. THERE ARE STAINS
ON THE SHAG CARPET, AND SINCE
THE WALLS ARE ALSO CARPETED,
THERE ARE STAINS ON THE WALLS,
TOO. I CAN'T EXACTLY FIGURE
OUT ALL THESE STAINS. MAYBE
THE SOVIETS NEVER DEVISED AN

EFFECTIVE STAIN REMOVAL TECH-
NOLOGY. MAYBE, IN THE END,
THAT'S WHAT FINISHED THEM OFF.
I MEAN, IT'S HARD TO MAKE A
CASE FOR A POLITICAL SYSTEM
THAT CAN'T GET THE STAINS OUT.

THE NEXT DAY IS SUNNY, AND
EVERYONE IN ZAGREB IS SIT-
TING AT TABLES IN THE STREET,
DRINKING BEER AND SMOKING.
THE TABLES ALL LOOK THE SAME
TO ME, BUT TOMISLAV EXPLAINS
THAT EACH RESTAURANT ALONG
THE STREET CONTROLS A
CERTAIN SECTION. I CAN'T TELL
WHERE ONE SECTION ENDS AND
ANOTHER BEGINS, BUT TOMISLAV
CAN, AND HE CHOOSES A TABLE
WHERE HE SAYS THE BEER IS
GOOD AND CHEAP.

ZAGREB ISN'T A BIG TOWN, BUT IT'S
GOT MORE THAN ITS FAIR SHARE OF

TWISTY STREETS STACKED WITH WORN-OUT BUILDINGS; ELEGANT BUILDINGS THAT ARE FADED AND CRACKED AND THAT COULD USE A FRESH COAT OF PAINT. THE WHOLE CITY IS SLIGHTLY DILAPIDATED. ON A DRIZZLY DAY, IT LOOKS EXACTLY THE WAY A CITY IN THE OLD YUGO-SLAVIA SHOULD: A CITY WHERE INTERNATIONAL SPIES DRINK THEMSELVES TO DEATH IN DARK APARTMENTS, AND WHERE EVERY LOVE AFFAIR ENDS IN AWKWARD SILENCE AND CIGAR-ETTE SMOKE.

THE CINEMA WHERE TOMISLAV WORKS IS CALLED THE K.I.C., WHICH IS PRONOUNCED "KISH" OR MAYBE "KITSCH." IT'S AN ACRONYM FOR SOMETHING. I NEVER

FIND OUT WHAT. TOMISLAV INTRODUCES ME TO THE PROJECTIONIST, AN OLD COMMUNIST WHO'S BEEN PROJECTING MOVIES SINCE THE DAYS WHEN CROATIA WAS JUST ANOTHER PART OF YUGOSLAVIA. I'M SO EXCITED THAT A SOVIET-ERA PROJECTIONIST IS PROJECTING MY MOVIES WITH A SOVIET-ERA PROJECTOR THAT I DON'T EVEN MIND THAT THE PICTURE IS FUZZY AND THE SOUND IS MUFFLED. AFTERWARD, TOMISLAV SEEMS A LITTLE UPSET THAT ONLY THREE PEOPLE SHOWED UP FOR THE SCREENING — AND THAT TWO OF THEM WALKED OUT MIDWAY THROUGH. I DON'T KNOW HOW TO EXPLAIN TO HIM THAT TONIGHT, I FEEL LIKE THE LUCKIEST GUY IN YUGOSLAVIA.

Cappy

THE BILLBOARD ADS FOR CAPPY ORANGE JUICE ARE PARTLY IN ENGLISH. "DON'T WORRY, BE CAPPY," THEY SAY. AFTER ONE SIP OF THE STUFF, IT'S OBVIOUS THIS IS A BAD TRANSLATION. THE ADS SHOULD SAY "DON'T WORRY, IT'S CRAPPY." THE STUFF IS MADE BY THE COCA-COLA CORPORATION. MAYBE COKE IS JUST GIVING CROATIANS WHAT THEY WANT, AND WHAT THEY WANT IS A WATERED-DOWN, VAGUELY CITRIC ORANGE-COLORED LIQUID. I BUY A CARTON OF CAPPY TO FIGHT THE EFFECTS OF THE TOMISLAV BEER I WAS DRINKING LAST NIGHT. TOMISLAV TELLS ME THAT BOTH HE AND THE BEER ARE NAMED

FOR THE 10TH-CENTURY KING WHO
FOUNDED CROATIA. I'M NOT SUR-
PRISED. THIS COUNTRY HAS A
LONG HISTORICAL MEMORY. IN
CROATIA, YOU CAN EVEN BLAME
YOUR HANGOVER ON HISTORY — OR,
AT LEAST, ON THE HISTORICAL
FIGURE YOUR BEER IS NAMED AFTER.
PEOPLE IN THE OLD YUGOSLAVIA
KNOW THEIR HISTORY, AND THEY
KNOW HOW TO HOLD A GRUDGE.
THESE TWO THINGS ARE NOT
UNRELATED. DURING THE CIVIL
WAR IN THE 1990's, THE PRESS
WAS ALWAYS MAKING A POINT OF
THIS: THAT PEOPLE IN THE
BALKANS WEREN'T JUST FIGHTING
THEIR PRESENT WAR, BUT WERE
FIGHTING ALL THEIR OLD WARS,
TOO. I GUESS THIS IS ONE WAY IN
WHICH AMERICANS ARE LUCKY.

SINCE NO ONE EXCEPT A FEW
DORKY CIVIL WAR RE-ENACTORS
COULD CARE LESS ABOUT HISTORY,
HISTORY IS THE ONE THING
AMERICANS DON'T FIGHT ABOUT.

LAST NIGHT, TOMISLAV TOOK ME
OUT FOR A DRINK. I ASK
HIM A MILLION QUESTIONS ABOUT
CROATIA, AND ABOUT THE WAR
IN THE 90's. I EXPECT HIM TO
SAY THAT THE WAR WAS SHITTY
AND THAT POLITICIANS ARE
CYNICAL AND THAT NATIONALISM
SUCKS. BUT HE DOESN'T SAY
THAT. INSTEAD, HE SAYS IT WAS
NECESSARY FOR CROATIA TO BE
HARD — THAT'S THE WORD HE USES —
BECAUSE THAT WAS THE ONLY
WAY FOR IT TO GAIN ITS
INDEPENDENCE. HE TELLS ME A
LITTLE ABOUT THE WAR. HOW
THE SERBS DROPPED BOMBS ON

ZAGREB. THEY USED CLUSTER BOMBS, WHICH SPRINKLE LITTLE BOMBLETS DOWN ON THE CITY LIKE AN ESPECIALLY LETHAL HAIL STORM. TOMISLAV WAS IN FILM SCHOOL AT THE TIME. ONE OF THE BOMBS BLEW UP A FIRST-YEAR STUDENT. ANOTHER BOMB BLEW UP A BUNCH OF BALLERINAS. WHAT TOMISLAV DOESN'T MENTION ARE THE WAR CRIMES. FROM WHAT I'VE READ, CROATIA WASN'T TOTALLY GUILTLESS IN THAT DEPARTMENT. MAYBE THAT'S WHAT TOMISLAV MEANS ABOUT BEING "HARD." BUT I DON'T ASK.

HALFWAY THROUGH MY SECOND GLASS OF TOMISLAV BEER, TWO THINGS HIT ME: THAT THIS IS NO ORDINARY BEER, AND THAT I CAN BARELY STAND UP. I STARE AT THE STUFF WITH A MIXTURE OF

FASCINATION AND DREAD. A BIG GLASS OF THICK BLACK POISON THAT BELCHES UP TOXIC BROWN BUBBLES. I TRY TO MAKE SOME ANALOGY BETWEEN BEER AND HISTORICAL MEMORY. HOW AMERICAN BEER — BUD LITE, FOR INSTANCE — IS WATERY AND CLEAR AND UNCOMPLICATED, WHILE THIS CROATIAN STUFF IS DARK AND DEADLY. BUT AT THIS POINT, I'M HAVING TROUBLE FORMING SENTENCES. I THINK THERE'S SOME MORE DRINKING, AND THEN SOMEHOW WE WIND UP AT AN AFTER-HOURS CASINO, WHICH LOOKS MORE LIKE THE SET FOR AN EASTERN EUROPEAN MAFIA MOVIE THAN A CASINO. THERE ARE BULKY MEN IN POLY-ESTER SUITS AND A FEW DROWSY PROSTITUTES LEANING AGAINST THE BAR. THERE AREN'T ANY ROULETTE WHEELS OR JACKPOT

SOUND EFFECTS. NONE OF THE RAZZLE-
DAZZLE STUFF THAT LAS VEGAS
CASINOS USE TO CONVINCE YOU
YOU'RE HAVING A REALLY GOOD
TIME. THIS CASINO DOESN'T
SEEM TO CARE TOO MUCH IF YOU'RE
HAVING A GOOD TIME, AND IN
FACT WOULD PROBABLY PREFER
THAT YOU WEREN'T. I DRINK A
BOTTLE OF COKE, TRYING DESP-
ERATELY TO WASH THE BLACK
POISON OF THAT THOUSAND-YEAR-
OLD CROATIAN KING OUT OF MY
SKULL. A DANGEROUS-LOOKING
GUY WHO'S MISSING A FEW TEETH
KEEPS GIVING ME HIGH-FIVES.
I HAVE NO IDEA WHY. NEXT THING
I KNOW, IT'S MORNING, AND MY
HEAD HURTS.

ANY TIME IS BUREK TIME!

TOMISLAV ASKS ME IF I WANT TO TRY SOME BUREK. IT'S A CROATIAN DISH. OKAY, I SAY.

WE GO TO AN ANCIENT FOOD STALL NEAR THE OUTDOOR MARKET. AN OLD LADY HANDS US TWO PLATES HEAPED WITH BUREK. SHE DOES NOT SAY "HAVE A NICE DAY," OR "ENJOY." IN FACT, THE EXPRESSION ON HER FACE SUGGESTS THAT SHE'D LIKE TO SAY "TAKE THIS BUREK AND SHOVE IT UP YOUR ASS."

BUREK IS BASICALLY FRIED POTATOES WITH BITS OF BONE WHITE CHEESE. IT'S REALLY SALTY. TOMISLAV GRABS A BIG BOWL OF SUGAR OFF THE COUNTER AND SPRINKLES SOME ON MY BUREK. THAT'S HOW THE LOCALS EAT IT, HE TELLS ME. "IT'S CROATIAN SOUL FOOD," HE SAYS.

TITO IS DEAD

BEFORE I LEAVE TOWN, TOMISLAV
TAKES ME TO SEE A DOCUMENTARY
ABOUT YUGOSLAVIA'S PUNK ROCK
SCENE. A LOT OF GOOD BANDS
CAME OUT OF ZAGREB AND
BELGRADE IN THE EARLY-1980's:
EKATERINA VELIKA, PRLJAVO
KAZALISTE, ELEKTRICNI ORGAZAM.
AFTER THE MOVIE, WE GO TO THE
LITTLE COFFEE SHOP WHERE THE
PUNKS USED TO HANG OUT. IT'S
OLD SCHOOL, THAT PLACE. NOT
OLD SCHOOL PUNK, BUT OLD
SCHOOL YUGOSLAVIA: A DINGY
LITTLE ROOM WHERE THE YEAR
1953 IS STILL HANGING OUT,
DRINKING WEAK COFFEE AND
TUNING INTO VOICE OF AMERICA
ON AN AM-RADIO. A COFFEE SHOP
THAT STILL HASN'T GOTTEN WORD
THAT THE COLD WAR IS OVER
AND TITO IS DEAD. THERE

AREN'T ANY TABLES OR CHAIRS
IN THE PLACE. IT'S MOSTLY JUST
AN EMPTY ROOM, WITH A COUPLE
THICKLY VARNISHED COUNTERS
AGAINST THE WALL, AND A
COFFEE BAR IN THE CORNER WITH
AN OLD LADY STANDING BEHIND
IT, GIVING TOMISLAV AND ME
THE EVIL EYE. IT'S HARD TO
BELIEVE THIS PLACE USED TO BE
THE EPICENTER OF THE ZAGREB
PUNK SCENE. BUT I JUST SAW A
MOVIE AND THIS PLACE WAS IN
IT, THIS VERY PLACE, OVERFLOW-
ING WITH PUNK ROCK KIDS. KIDS
PRESSED AGAINST THE WINDOWS.
KIDS SPILLING OUT ONTO THE
SIDEWALK. BUT NOW THE KIDS
ARE GONE, AND THIS PLACE
PROBABLY LOOKS EXACTLY LIKE
IT LOOKED BEFORE THEY
SHOWED UP: DREARY AND HOPELESS.

LIKE THE LAST PLACE IN THE
WORLD WHERE ANYTHING FUN
WOULD EVER HAPPEN.

AFTER I'VE LEFT TOWN, I REALIZE
I NEVER ASKED TOMISLAV WHY
THE PUNK KIDS CHOSE THAT
COFFEE SHOP IN THE FIRST PLACE.
I WONDER IF THEY FELL IN LOVE
WITH IT, FOR THE SAME REASON
I'VE FALLEN IN LOVE WITH ALL
SORTS OF OLD DINERS AND
COFFEE SHOPS. BECAUSE THOSE
ARE THE PLACES WHERE THE
PAST SHOWS UP LIKE A LONG
LOST FRIEND. LIKE THE RISEN
DEAD.

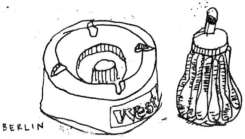

BERLIN

DRESDEN

IN DRESDEN, I SLEEP ON BASTIAN'S
FLOOR. BASTIAN IS 8 OR 9
FEET TALL AND RAIL THIN, THE
WAY ALL THESE GERMAN KIDS
ARE. HE'S ALSO A NICE GUY,
AND ONE MORNING, HE TAKES
ME ON A BIKE TOUR OF THE CITY.
DRESDEN IS IN WHAT USED TO
BE EAST GERMANY, WHICH
MAKES EVERYTHING COMPLICATED.
TAKE THE FRAUENKIRCHE, FOR
INSTANCE. IT WAS A CHURCH
THAT WAS MOSTLY REDUCED TO
RUBBLE WHEN DRESDEN WAS
FIREBOMBED AT THE END OF
W.W. 2. DURING THE COMMUNIST
DAYS, THE RUINS SERVED AS
A READY-MADE MEMORIAL:
TO THE WAR, AND TO THE DEAD,

BUT ALSO TO THE FACT THAT THE
PAST CAN'T BE RECLAIMED
SIMPLY BY REBUILDING IT.
BUT NOW GERMANY IS REUNIFIED,
AND DRESDEN IS BUILDING A
NEW, HISTORICALLY ACCURATE
FRAUENKIRCHE. PRETTY SOON,
NO ONE WILL EVEN REMEMBER
THE RUINED, COMMUNIST-ERA
VERSION OF THE CHURCH.
BASTIAN TELLS ME THIS IS PART
OF A BIGGER PLAN, AT LEAST
AMONG WEST GERMANS: TO
PRETEND EAST GERMANY NEVER
HAPPENED. ANOTHER IDEA,
BASTIAN TELLS ME, IS TO RE-
CREATE DRESDEN'S OLD, PRE-
COMMUNIST STREET GRID; TO
RESTORE THE CITY'S OLD
DIMENSIONS, EVEN IF IT'S
MISSING MOST OF ITS OLD

BUILDINGS. BASTIAN AND I RIDE ALONG THE WIDE, AXIAL STREETS OF THE COMMUNIST CITY, THE LONG SIGHTLINES ALREADY INTERRUPTED BY NEW BUILDINGS. IT'S A COMPLICATED THING DRESDEN WANTS TO DO: TO REPLACE THE CITY THE COMMUNISTS BUILT WITH A BRAND NEW, OLD CITY, THAT SOMEHOW BOTH PRE-DATES AND POST-DATES THE EAST GERMAN ERA. TO THE PEOPLE CURRENTLY IN CHARGE, THE COMMUNIST CITY WAS NEVER THE 'REAL' DRESDEN, ANY MORE THAN THE RUINED FRAUENKIRCHE WAS THE 'REAL' FRAUENKIRCHE. AND IF THE COMMUNIST CITY WASN'T REAL, NEITHER WAS ITS HISTORY, OR EVEN ITS CITIZENS, FOR THAT MATTER. BASTIAN

TELLS ME THIS IS WHAT'S ACTUALLY BEHIND THE BAD FEELINGS BETWEEN WESSIES AND OSSIES. IT'S NOT THAT THE OSSIES WANT THEIR CRAPPY OLD POLITICAL SYSTEM BACK. THEY JUST DON'T WANT THEIR OLD LIVES TOSSED INTO THE TRASH HEAP OF HISTORY ALONG WITH THE OLD REGIME. AND BESIDES, THERE ARE THINGS ABOUT THE COMMUNIST CITY THAT ARE REALLY COOL. THAT SILVER-SKINNED DEPARTMENT STORE DOWN-TOWN, FOR INSTANCE. YEAH, THERE MAY HAVE ONLY BEEN SCARCITY FOR SALE INSIDE. BUT FROM OUTSIDE, I CAN IMAGINE COSMONAUTS PULLING UP IN ROCKET CARS AND GOING IN TO BUY TRENDY SPACE HELMETS. "IT LOOKS LIKE IT WAS BUILT BY SPACE ALIENS," BASTIAN SAYS. "OR SWEDISH ARCHITECTS," I

SAY. "SAME DIFFERENCE,"
BASTIAN SAYS.

BERLIN — A woman doing handsprings hurled herself into two art installations at the controversial exhibition of a collection belonging to the billionaire heir of a Nazi-era arms supplier, damaging both pieces, organizers said Thursday.

The bizarre attack came late Wednesday on the top floor of the Hamburger Bahnhof museum, where Friedrich Christian Flick's collection was opened to the public earlier in the day.

Yelling loudly, the 35-year-old woman attacked "Office Baroque," a cutout section of wall by American artist Gordon Matta-Clark, doing a series of head-over-heels flips before landing on the work in a handstand, punching both her arms through the drywall, said Klaus Dieter Lehmann, president of Berlin's Prussian Cultural Heritage Foundation.

Ⓐ 45¢ PEE.

WHEN YOU BOARD A TRAIN IN GERMANY, CHANCES ARE YOU'LL WIND UP IN A COMPARTMENT SITTING KNEE-TO-KNEE ACROSS FROM A STRANGER. AND CHANCES ARE THIS STRANGER WON'T MAKE EYE CONTACT WITH YOU, LET ALONE SAY HELLO. THIS RESERVE SEEMS A LITTLE EXTREME TO THE AMERICAN PART OF ME; THE PART THAT THINKS SILENCE AMONG STRANGERS, ESPECIALLY STRANGERS WHOSE KNEES ARE TOUCHING YOURS, IS UNNATURAL. IT TAKES ME A WHILE TO GET USED TO THIS SILENCE. NOW I'M A BIG FAN. I MEAN, WHEN YOU'RE CRAMMED INTO CLOSE QUARTERS ON A TRAIN, IT'S PRETTY DECENT OF YOUR FELLOW TRAVELERS NOT TO BE ANNOYING BLABBERMOUTHS. AND BESIDES, FOR EVERY TIME A

GERMAN PERSON DOESN'T SAY
HELLO TO YOU, THEY'RE SURE TO
SAY GOODBYE. YOU CAN BE
LOCKED IN A LITTLE TRAIN
COMPARTMENT WITH A GERMAN
PERSON, AND 5 OR 10 HOURS WILL
PASS IN TOTAL SILENCE. BUT
WHEN THIS PERSON FINALLY GETS
UP TO LEAVE, THEY'LL ALWAYS
PAUSE BY THE DOOR AND TURN
AROUND AND SAY "TSCHUSS,"
WHICH MEANS "SO LONG." AS
IF THIS IS WHAT'S WORTH
ACKNOWLEDGING: NOT THE HOURS
SPENT TRAVELING WITH
STRANGERS, BUT THE BRIEF,
POIGNANT MOMENT OF SAYING
GOODBYE TO THEM.
I'M THINKING ABOUT THIS WHILE
I'M SITTING IN A LITTLE
RESTAURANT IN PRENZLAUER
BERG. ACTUALLY, I'M THINKING

ABOUT ALL THE MONEY I'VE SPENT TAKING PEES IN GERMANY. USING A PUBLIC TOILET IN EUROPE USUALLY COSTS YOU SOMETHING, AND WHEN THE SUPPLY IS LOW AND THE DEMAND IS HIGH, IT CAN GET PRETTY PRICEY. AT THE FRIEDRICHSTRASSE TRAIN STATION IN BERLIN, FOR INSTANCE, A PEE COSTS 80 CENTS. THAT'S WHEN YOU START THINKING ABOUT MATTERS OF QUALITY. YOU ASK YOURSELF IF YOUR LAST PEE WAS REALLY WORTH 80 CENTS, AND YOU START FEELING JEALOUS OF PEOPLE WITH BIG BLADDERS WHO ARE GETTING MUCH BETTER VALUE FOR THEIR MONEY THAN YOU ARE. ANYWAY, THAT'S ACTUALLY WHAT I'M THINKING ABOUT WHEN A COUPLE GERMAN

KIDS ASK IF THEY CAN SIT AT
MY TABLE BECAUSE THERE'S NO
WHERE ELSE TO SIT. THE
TABLE IS SMALL, SO WE HAVE
TO SIT PRETTY CLOSE, EATING
ELBOW TO ELBOW. THE GERMAN
KIDS PRETTY MUCH IGNORE ME
TILL THEY GET UP TO LEAVE.
THEN THEY SMILE AND SAY
"TSCHUSS," AND I SMILE AND
SAY "TSCHUSS," TOO, AND I
FEEL A LITTLE SAD TO SEE
THEM GO.

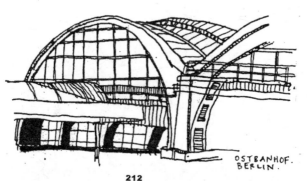

OSTBANHOF.
BERLIN.

MAY DAY

IT'S MAY 1ST IN BERLIN, WHICH
MEANS THE FLOWERS ARE OUT
AND SO ARE THE COPS. NORMALLY,
BERLIN IS A PRETTY SLEEPY
CITY, BUT TODAY THE SKY IS
BUZZING WITH BLACK MILITARY
HELICOPTERS, AND THE STREETS
ARE FULL OF THE CLUNKY GREEN-
AND-WHITE VW BUSES THAT THE
POLICE DRIVE. IT'S HARD TO
TAKE A POLICE FORCE THAT
DRIVES AROUND IN VW HIPPY VANS
SERIOUSLY, TILL YOU NOTICE
THE COPS INSIDE ARE WEARING
RIOT HELMETS AND CARRYING
SUB-MACHINE GUNS. THE POLICE
VANS DASH AROUND WITH THEIR
SIRENS BLARING. EE-AW, EE-AW.
THE CLASSIC, TWO-TONE 'EURO-

SIREN: A HIGH NOTE FOLLOWED BY A LOW NOTE. IT'S THE SOUND OF AN OLD BLACK-AND-WHITE MOVIE WITH SUBTITLES. A MOVIE WHERE A LOVE AFFAIR ENDS ON A RAIN-SLICKED AIRPORT TARMAC, AND IN THE DISTANCE, HEARTBREAK DISTILLED TO THE TWO TONES OF A POLICE SIREN. THOSE SIRENS ALWAYS CHOKE ME UP. MAYBE THAT'S THE POINT. TO MAKE THE CRIMINALS FEEL TOO MELANCHOLY AND HOPELESS TO PUT UP MUCH RESISTANCE WHEN THE COPS SHOW UP. BUT TODAY, THE COPS ARE OUT BE-CAUSE MAY DAY IS LIKE ANARCHIST CHRISTMAS: THE DAY ALL THE PUNK KIDS AND SKINHEADS OPEN UP THE CITY LIKE IT'S THE BEST PRESENT UNDER THE TREE.

I DECIDE TO TAKE A LONG WALK
ACROSS TOWN, MAKING MY WAY
OVER TO KARL-MARX ALLEE.
THE STREET IS AN ENDLESSLY
LONG SHOWCASE OF COMMUNIST-
ERA ARCHITECTURE THAT USED
TO BE CALLED STALIN ALLEE
UNTIL THE RUSSIANS DEMOTED
STALIN FROM SAINT TO ASSHOLE.
MY FAVORITE PART OF THE
STREET IS NEAR ALEXANDERPLATZ.
THE BUILDINGS ARE MOSTLY
FROM THE 1960's, MODERNIST
AND SORT OF KITSCHY. THERE'S
AN OLD RESTAURANT CALLED THE
MOSCOW CAFE THAT PROBABLY
WENT OUT OF BUSINESS THE DAY
AFTER THE WALL CAME DOWN.
IT LOOKS LIKE A DENNY'S IN
A PARALLEL, COMMUNIST UNIVERSE.

ON ONE OF THE WALLS, THERE'S A MOSAIC THAT DEPICTS SMILING PEOPLE FROM ALL OVER THE SOVIET EMPIRE: KAZAKS AND UZBEKS AND CAUCASIANS. A BRIGHT, SUNNY IMAGE OF INTER-NATIONAL COMMUNISM TO GREET YOU BEFORE YOU TUCK INTO A GRAND SLAM BREAKFAST OF BLINIS AND VODKA. NEXT TO THE RESTAURANT IS A SIGN POLE TOPPED BY A SILVERY ORB WITH THREE ANTENNAS POKING OUT OF IT. A FAKE SPUTNIK. SPUTNIK ON A STICK. I FEEL A LITTLE SAD FOR THAT FAKE SATELLITE. IT PROBABLY WISHES IT WERE SOARING TOWARD THE STARS. INSTEAD, IT'S STUCK ON TOP OF A SIGN POLE NEXT TO A SHUTTERED RESTAURANT IN A

CITY THAT ISN'T EAST BERLIN ANYMORE:

MY TRAIL OF SHATTERED EAST GERMAN DREAMS ENDS AT THE PALAST DER REPUBLIK. THERE USED TO BE A SCHMALTZY BAROQUE PALACE ON THE SITE CALLED THE BERLIN SCHLOSS. IT GOT BOMBED DURING THE WAR. A LOT OF PEOPLE SAID IT COULD HAVE BEEN RESTORED, BUT THE EAST GERMANS INSISTED THAT THE PLACE WAS BEYOND REDEMP-TION. MAYBE THEY WEREN'T TALKING ABOUT THE PALACE IT-SELF, BUT EVERYTHING THE PALACE STOOD FOR — AND ANYWAY, WHAT'S A BRAVE NEW COMMUNIST CITY NEED WITH A MUSTY OLD ROYAL PALACE? IN THE END, THEY BLEW

THE THING TO SMITHEREENS. THE
SITE SAT VACANT FOR YEARS,
TILL THE MID-70's, WHEN THE
COMMUNISTS BUILT THE PALACE
OF THE REPUBLIC. THE BUILDING
IS A HUGE MODERNIST BLOCK
WITH ACRES OF BRONZE-COLORED
MIRRORED WINDOWS; A NEW
KIND OF PALACE FOR A NEW
KIND OF STATE — AT LEAST, THAT'S
WHAT THE EAST GERMAN AUTHOR-
ITIES HAD IN MIND. BUT BY 1976,
NO ONE IN EAST BERLIN WAS
BUYING IT. AFTER THE WALL FELL,
THE NEW BERLIN GOVERNMENT
ANNOUNCED PLANS TO BULLDOZE
THE PALACE OF THE REPUBLIC.
THIS MADE A LOT OF EAST BERLIN-
ERS MAD. SURE, THE COMMUNISTS
SUCKED, BUT THE PALACE HAD
ACTUALLY BEEN PRETTY FUN,

SORT OF THE PARTY HOUSE OF THE
PEOPLE. THERE WAS A BOWLING
ALLEY AND A DISCO. PEOPLE
WENT THERE ON DATES. IN 1980,
'TANGERINE DREAM' PLAYED A
COUPLE SHOWS THERE, THE FIRST
WESTERN ROCK BAND TO PLAY IN
EAST GERMANY. THE WESSIES
WANT TO BULLDOZE THE OLD
COMMUNIST PALACE FOR THE SAME
REASON THE OSSIES BULLDOZED
THE OLD ROYAL PALACE: TO IN-
AUGURATE A NEW REGIME; TO
EXORCISE OLD GHOSTS. BUT TO
THE OSSIES, THIS IS JUST ANOTHER
INSTANCE OF WESSIE INSENSITIVITY.
AND IT GETS WEIRDER. AMONG THE
PEOPLE WHO WANT TO KNOCK DOWN
THE PALACE IS A VOCAL FACTION
WHO WANT TO REBUILD THE OLD
PALACE, THE BERLIN SCHLOSS.

NO ONE CAN SAY WHAT BERLIN
NEEDS A HUGE BAROQUE ROYAL
PALACE FOR, ESPECIALLY SINCE
THE LAST KAISER KICKED THE
BUCKET A CENTURY AGO, BUT
THAT'S THE IDEA.

WHEN I GET TO THE PALACE OF
THE REPUBLIC, I'M SURPRISED
TO FIND SOMETHING GOING ON
INSIDE: AN EXHIBITION OF
QIN DYNASTY TERRA COTTA SOLDIERS.
THE SOLDIERS, IT TURNS OUT, ARE
JUST REPLICAS. THIS GIVES ME
AN IDEA. IF THEY DO DECIDE TO
BUILD A REPLICA OF THE OLD
ROYAL PALACE, THIS IS WHAT
THEY COULD USE IT FOR: NOT
EXHIBITIONS OF ART, BUT EXHIB-
ITIONS OF ART REPLICAS. A
PHONY PALACE FULL OF PHONY ART.

TRENO TO NAPOLI

I FALL ASLEEP ON A ZUG LEAVING
MÜNCHEN AND WAKE UP ON A
TRENO ROLLING INTO NAPOLI.
MY DREAMS LAST NIGHT WERE
SEXY DREAMS. DREAMS ABOUT
DREAM LOVERS. MAYBE THAT'S
WHAT EVERYONE ON THIS ITALIAN
TRAIN IS DREAMING ABOUT. IN
FACT, MAYBE THAT'S WHY THIS
TRAIN IS SO PACKED. BECAUSE
THE DREAMS YOU HAVE ON ITALIAN
TRAINS ARE TRIPLE-X. GERMAN
TRAINS AREN'T USUALLY SO FULL,
AND MOST PEOPLE ARE READING
BOOKS INSTEAD OF NODDING OFF.
MAYBE THAT'S BECAUSE THE
DREAMS ARE DIFFERENT ON GERMAN
TRAINS. YOU DREAM GLASS AND
STEEL DREAMS, AS PRECISE AS
AN ARCHITECT'S MEASURED

DRAWING. YOU DREAM OF CITIES MADE OF CUT GLASS AND OF THE TRAINS THAT GLIDE SOUNDLESSLY THROUGH THEM. THESE DREAMS ARE LONELY, SO PEOPLE MOSTLY STAY AWAKE, STARING OUT THE WINDOW AT THE NEARLY PERFECT GERMAN CITIES THAT PASS OUTSIDE THE NEARLY PERFECT GERMAN TRAINS. BUT ITALIAN TRAIN DREAMS ARE PURE SMUT, AND EVERYONE IS EAGER TO DOZE OFF.

THE FIRST THING I DO IN NAPLES IS GET A CUP OF COFFEE. I FIND A COFFEE BAR ON A SIDE STREET. IT'S DEFINITELY NOT A FANCY PLACE, BUT THE GUY AT THE ESPRESSO MACHINE IS WEARING A FANCY UNIFORM. THIS REMINDS ME OF SOMETHING SERGIO TOLD

ME: THAT ITALIANS LIKE UNIFORMS.
WE'RE NOT TALKING POLYESTER
McDONALD'S-STYLE UNIFORMS
THAT MAKE YOU FEEL BAD FOR THE
PEOPLE WHO HAVE TO WEAR THEM,
BUT FANCY UNIFORMS: NAVY
BLUE JACKETS AND BLEACHY
WHITE SHIRTS WITH GOLD EPAULETS.
UNIFORMS THAT MAKE EVERY
TRAFFIC COP OR COFFEE SHOP GUY
LOOK LIKE A MOVIE STAR OR A
HEAD-OF-STATE. WHEN THE GUY
MAKING MY COFFEE WEARS A
UNIFORM LIKE THAT, I HAVE
MIXED FEELINGS. ON THE ONE
HAND, THE UNIFORM MAKES ME
FEEL CONFIDENT THAT MY
CAPPUCCINO WILL BE CRAFTED
WITH MILITARY PRECISION. ON THE
OTHER HAND, THE FACT THAT
MOST OF THESE COFFEE GUYS ARE

SURLY MAKES GETTING A COFFEE
FEEL MORE LIKE GETTING A
SPEEDING TICKET OR A COURT
MARTIAL.

OUT ON THE STREET, IT'S ALL
CHAOTIC AND CRAZY. NAPLES IS
A CITY THAT MAKES A BIG
PRODUCTION OUT OF BEING A CITY,
FULL OF PEOPLE MAKING A BIG
PRODUCTION OUT OF BEING ALIVE.
IT'S PROBABLY NOT IMPOSSIBLE
TO BE MELANCHOLY HERE, BUT
SOMEWHERE ALONG THE WAY,
YOU'RE SURE TO GET DISTRACTED:
ALMOST RUN OVER BY A VESPA
OR HASSLED BY SOME BAD-ASS
SCHOOL KIDS; OR YOU'LL EAT A
CUP OF COCONUT GELATO OR FALL
IN LOVE WITH A CUTE ITALIAN
GIRL, AND AFTER THAT, HOW
CAN YOU STAY DEPRESSED? EVEN

SO, AFTER A COUPLE DAYS, I START
HAVING VIOLENT FANTASIES IN
WHICH EVERY OBNOXIOUS KID ON
A MOTOR SCOOTER COLLIDES WITH
EVERY KAMIKAZE TAXI CAB,
AND THE WREAKAGE PILES HIGH
OVER THE CITY LIKE A SECOND
VESUVIUS. THESE THOUGHTS
FILL ME WITH A SOCIOPATHIC
SENSE OF SERENITY WHICH IS
EITHER THE FIRST SIGN THAT I'M
GOING NATIVE, OR THE FIRST
SIGN THAT I NEVER WILL.

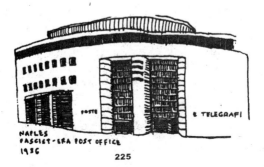

POSTE

E TELEGRAFI

NAPLES
FASCIST-ERA POST OFFICE
1936

THE CREVICE AND OTHER WONDERS

THE 1968 EARTHQUAKE IN THE BELICE VALLEY WASN'T ONE OF SICILY'S FINER MOMENTS. THE EARTHQUAKE WIPED OUT MOST OF THE VALLEY'S LITTLE 17TH CENTURY VILLAGES AND A LOT OF PEOPLE DIED. THEN THE TROUBLE BEGAN. THE GOVERNMENT'S RELIEF EFFORT WAS A NATURAL DISASTER OF ITS OWN. WHAT THE GOVERNMENT DIDN'T BUNGLE, THE MAFIA STOLE. LOTS OF RELIEF MONEY GOT POURED INTO BOGUS RECONSTRUCTION PROJECTS. ONE OF THE WAYS THE MAFIA LAUNDERS ITS MONEY IS THROUGH CONSTRUCTION PROJECTS NOBODY NEEDS AND THAT NEVER GET FINISHED. THERE'S EVEN A WORD FOR THE PRACTICE :

ABUSIVISMO. YOU SEE THE RESULTS
ALL OVER THE PLACE : HALF-
BUILT CONCRETE SKELETONS WITH
A RUSTING CONSTRUCTION CRANE
HANGING OVERHEAD; BUILDINGS
IN RUINS BEFORE THEY EVEN HAD
A CHANCE TO BE BUILDINGS.
AFTER THE EARTHQUAKE, THE
GOVERNMENT DECIDED THAT THE
OLD VILLAGES WEREN'T WORTH
REPAIRING. INSTEAD, THEY BUILT
BRAND-NEW REPLACEMENT TOWNS.
I READ SOMEWHERE THAT THE
DESIGN OF THE NEW TOWNS WAS
BASED ON 'UTOPIAN PRINCIPLES.'
APPARENTLY, THOSE PRINCIPLES
INCLUDED OVERSIZED WIND-SWEPT
PLAZAS, AND ABSTRACT PUBLIC
ART, AND OCEANS OF CONCRETE.
I READ THAT IN ONE OF THE TOWNS,

NEW GIBELLINA, "NO BLOCK CAN HAVE MORE THAN ONE COMMERCIAL OUTLET, BECAUSE THE ARCHITECTS FELT THAT DOWNTOWN AREAS WERE A TOOL OF SUBTLE CAPITALIST HEGEMONY." EVEN WEIRDER THAN NEW GIBELLINA, THOUGH, IS WHAT HAPPENED TO OLD GIBELLINA. NOT LONG AFTER THE '68 QUAKE, A TUSCAN SCULPTOR NAMED ALBERTO BURRI SOMEHOW CONVINCED THE GOVERNMENT THAT IT'D BE PRETTY COOL TO ENCASE THE RUINS OF THE OLD TOWN IN CONCRETE. THE RESULT IS A SLIGHTLY MIND-BOGGLING PIECE OF ART BURRI CALLED IL CRETTO — THE CREVICE. BURRI PRESERVED THE OLD STREET GRID, SO YOU CAN STILL WALK THROUGH THE OLD VILLAGE. BUT

NOW, INSTEAD OF SHOPS AND HOUSES, THE STREETS ARE LINED WITH A CONTINUOUS WALL OF CONCRETE THAT'S JUST ABOUT AS TALL AS YOU ARE. A LOT OF PEOPLE WEREN'T TOO HAPPY ABOUT BURRI'S PROJECT, BUT IF YOU ASK ME, IT WAS BETTER THAN USING THE CONCRETE TO BUILD YET ANOTHER VAST, WINDY PLAZA IN SOME CREEPY NEW TOWN. AT LEAST BURRI INTENDED TO BUILD A GHOST TOWN. WHEN THOSE UTOPIAN ARCHITECTS DID THE SAME THING, IT WAS JUST AN ACCIDENT OF BAD DESIGN.

ON MONDAY MORNING, I DRIVE MY RENTAL CAR BACK TO PALERMO. THIS IS A MISTAKE. DRIVING INTO PALERMO DURING THE MONDAY MORNING RUSH HOUR

ISN'T LIKE DRIVING SO MUCH AS IT'S LIKE TRYING TO CARRY TWO PLASTIC CUPS FULL OF BEER THROUGH A MOSH PIT FULL OF SKINHEAD SPEED FREAKS. THERE AREN'T ANY LANES. THERE AREN'T ANY RULES. THERE'S JUST TRAFFIC, AND THE IMPOSSIBILITY OF PREDICTING THE TRAJECTORY OF SO MANY MOVING OBJECTS — IMPOSSIBLE, UNLESS YOU'RE EITHER A TOP SECRET PENTAGON ANTI-MISSILE SUPERCOMPUTER, OR A SICILIAN WITH A COUPLE ESPRESSOS COURSING THROUGH YOUR BLOODSTREAM. SOMEHOW, MY CAR ROLLS THROUGH ALL THIS FLYING STEEL. IT'S A MIRACLE, BUT MAYBE THAT'S HOW SICILY OPERATES. ON MIRACLES. IT'D

EXPLAIN THE SHRINES YOU SEE ALL
OVER THE PLACE: LITTLE NICHES
ON THE CORNERS OF BUILDINGS
WITH A STATUE OF A SAINT
INSIDE. THE FANCIER SHRINES
ARE DECORATED WITH CHRISTMAS
LIGHTS, AND A FEW ARE EVEN
FRAMED BY BLUE NEON TUBES.
THOSE SHRINES ARE MY FAVORITE,
THE ONES THAT INEXPLICABLY
MIX THE AESTHETICS OF
SICILIAN CATHOLICISM AND
A ROUTE 66 MOTEL SIGN. IT
MAKES SENSE, SOMEHOW. BOTH
APPEAL TO THE SAME AUDIENCE.
THE SAME TIRED SOULS IN SEARCH
OF A LITTLE COMFORT. ANYWAY,
THE FACT THAT THESE LITTLE
SHRINES ARE AT ALMOST EVERY
INTERSECTION MAKES ME

SUSPECT THEY'VE GOT SOMETHING
TO DO WITH DRIVING IN THIS TOWN.
LIKE THEY'RE SUPERNATURAL TRAFFIC
SIGNALS. EVERYONE IGNORES
THE STOP SIGNS AND THE RED
LIGHTS, BUT WHO KNOWS? MAYBE
IT'S BECAUSE THEY'RE OBEYING
SOME HIGHER TRAFFIC
AUTHORITY.

MESSINA TRAIN STATION. SICILY.
I JUST MISSED THE TRAIN.

WHAT I DRANK AT THAT LITTLE CAFE ON THE ISLAND OF LIPARI (OFF THE COAST OF SICILY) WHILE WAITING FOR THE WIND TO DIE DOWN SO THE FERRIES CAN SAIL.

DAY 1. COKE.

THE WAITER SAYS
THE WIND IS COMING
FROM AFRICA.

DAY 2. BEER.
STILL WINDY.

(PEANUTS.)

DAY 3. BEER.

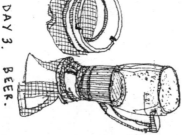

WIENER KLEINER BRÄUNER

ANOTHER NIGHT TRAIN TO VIENNA.
I WAKE UP JUST BEFORE DAWN
AS THE TRAIN WINDS SLOW AND
EASY THROUGH THE AUSTRIAN
ALPS. THE WINDOW IS OPEN A
CRACK, AND OUTSIDE, I CAN
HEAR THE MORNING BIRDS
CHIRPING. I START TO WONDER
IF THIS IS WHERE I'M HAPPIEST:
IN BETWEEN THE PLACE I'M
COMING FROM AND THE PLACE
I'M GOING. AND IT OCCURS TO ME
THAT THIS PROBABLY ISN'T THE
BEST PLACE TO FIND HAPPINESS,
BECAUSE IT'S NO PLACE AT ALL.

THIS TIME, WHEN I GET OFF THE
TRAIN IN VIENNA, I KNOW EXACTLY
WHERE TO FIND A CUP OF COFFEE.
I HEAD TO THE CAFE BRÄUNERHOF,

AN OLD COFFEE HOUSE IN AN OLD
PART OF TOWN. I ASK FOR A
KLEINER BRAÜNER, BITTE — A
LITTLE BLACK COFFEE, PLEASE.
IT COMES IN A WHITE CHINA CUP
ON A WHITE PAPER DOILY, DELIV-
ERED BY AN OLD WAITER IN A
BLACK TUXEDO WITH A BIG BOW
TIE. A CUP OF THE SAME
BLACK COFFEE THAT PERCOLATES
UP FROM BENEATH THIS CITY,
THE WAY OIL BUBBLES UP IN
WEST TEXAS. THE STRONG BLACK
DISTILLATE OF SO MANY DEAD
THINGS: OLD BONES; OLD CRIMES;
UNDANCED WALTZES; UNREQUITED
LOVE. VIENNA IS FULL OF COFFEE
HOUSES, ELEGANT PLACES, SOME
OF THEM, WITH CRYSTAL
CHANDELIERS AND MOSAIC TILES

ON THE CEILING. THE COFFEE IS RIDICULOUSLY GOOD, AND THE PRICE OF ADMISSION TO THESE LITTLE PALACES IS A CUP OF THE STUFF. THEN YOU'RE WELCOME to SPEND THE DAY SIPPING COFFEE AND READING THE PAPER WHILE A STONY-FACED WAITER SHUFFLES FROM TABLE TO TABLE, TAKING EACH ORDER WITH AN ALMOST UNDETECTABLE NOD. IN ITALY, YOU DON'T SIT DOWN. YOU STAND AT THE COFFEE BAR AND SLUG DOWN AN ESPRESSO OR TWO AND TAKE OFF. THE DIFFERENCE BETWEEN DRINKING COFFEE IN VIENNA AND DRINKING IT IN ITALY IS THE DIFFERENCE BETWEEN A SLOW-MO LIFE OF LONG PAUSES, AND A FAST-SPEED LIFE WHERE

XT MOMENT CAN'T COME
NOUGH. THERE'S SOME-
TO BE SAID FOR BOTH
OF LIFE, AND AS LONG
RE'S A NIGHT TRAIN
EN VIENNA AND ROME,
S ABSOLUTELY NO REASON
OOSE ONE OVER THE OTHER.

• EHI TÚ •

CERCO PASSAGGIO IN
AUTO X IL CONCERTO
DEI **KraftwerK**
a ROMA [LUNEDÍ 17/05]
CI ANDIAMO INSIEME?
DIVIDIAMO LE SPESE
EMILIANO
328-3886102

Sightseer

THE TOUR BOATS ON THE SEINE ARE A
MILE LONG. THEY'RE BARGES MORE
THAN BOATS, PACKED WITH SIGHT-
SEERS TRYING TO SQUARE THE
PARIS THEY'RE LOOKING AT WITH
THE PARIS IN THEIR HEADS.
THAT'S HOW IT IS WHEN YOU'RE A
TOURIST. YOU'RE ALWAYS ON THE
LOOK-OUT, PROWLING AROUND
WITH A LAMINATED MAP, OR A
DIGITAL VIDEO CAMERA, OR A
LITTLE PLASTIC AUDIO TOUR
TELEPHONE THAT WHISPERS THE
CITY'S SECRETS IN YOUR EAR.
YOU'RE ALWAYS LOOKING FOR THE
CITY THAT YOU DREAMED ABOUT,
OR AT LEAST A CITY THAT COMES
CLOSE. THE HUCKSTERS PREY
ON TOURISTS. CON ARTISTS WHO
PROMISE THEY CAN SHOW YOU

YOUR DREAM CITY IF YOU'LL JUST
HOP ABOARD THEIR DOUBLE-DECKER
TOUR BUS OR TAKE THEIR FULLY-
NARRATED-IN-FOUR-LANGUAGES
DELUXE RIVER CRUISE. YOU CAN
WASTE A LOT OF TIME AND
MONEY BEFORE YOU REALIZE
THOSE JERKS DON'T KNOW WHERE
THE CITY IS, EITHER.

MY ITALIAN PAL SERGIO HAS A
CRUSH ON PARIS. BACK IN HIS
APARTMENT IN GERMANY, HE'S
GOT A BIG MAP OF THE CITY
PINNED TO HIS WALL, CENTERFOLD-
STYLE. ONE NIGHT, I ASK HIM
HIS OPINION OF A COUPLE THEORIES
I HAVE ABOUT PARIS. THE FIRST
ONE INVOLVES COFFEE. IF
THERE'S SOMETHING IN PARIS
THAT'S THE EQUAL OF A VIENNESE

COFFEE HOUSE, I HAVEN'T FOUND IT.
"WHAT ABOUT THE CAFÉS?"
SERGIO ASKS, A LITTLE INDIGNANT.
YEAH, THE CAFÉS. THEY'RE
SUPPOSED TO BE WHAT PARIS IS
ALL ABOUT: A GOOD CAFÉ ON
SOME BOULEVARD; SPENDING
ALL DAY SIPPING COFFEE AND
SMOKING GAULOISES AT A LITTLE
TABLE ON THE SIDEWALK. THEN
YOU FIND OUT A COFFEE COSTS
6 BUCKS, AND THE WAITER GIVES
YOU ATTITUDE IF YOU SIT
THERE TOO LONG. SO MY FIRST
THEORY IS THAT YOU CAN TELL
WHAT A SOCIETY REALLY VALUES
BY THE STUFF IT KEEPS CHEAP.
IT'S THE STUFF THAT'S IMPORTANT
ENOUGH THAT ANYONE CAN
AFFORD IT. CAPPUCCINOS IN
ITALY, FOR INSTANCE, OR VODKA

IN RUSSIA, OR DOUBLE CHEESE
BURGERS IN THE U.S. CHEAP
STUFF IS WHAT A SOCIETY
DOESN'T CONSIDER LUXURIES BUT
STAPLES. BAGUETTES IN PARIS.
PIZZA SLICES IN NAPLES. BAGELS
IN MONTREAL. THE INVERSE OF
MY THEORY ALSO APPLIES: IF YOU
CAN'T AFFORD THE PRICE OF A
CUP OF COFFEE IN A PARISIAN
CAFÉ, FOR INSTANCE, THEN
MAYBE CAFÉ CULTURE ISN'T AS
IMPORTANT TO PARISIANS AS
PEOPLE CLAIM IT IS. SERGIO IS
SILENT. "BUT EVERYTHING IN
PARIS IS OVERPRICED," HE
FINALLY SAYS.

MY SECOND THEORY — OKAY, IT'S
ACTUALLY AN OBSERVATION — HAS
TO DO WITH THE METRO. I ASK

SERGIO IF HE'S EVER NOTICED THE
LITTLE WARNING SIGNS STUCK TO
THE DOORS OF THE PARIS SUB-
WAY. THE SIGNS WARN YOU IN
FOUR DIFFERENT LANGUAGES
NOT TO LEAN AGAINST THE DOOR.
I'VE NOTICED THAT THE ITALIAN
VERSION OF THESE WARNINGS
IS ALWAYS FOLLOWED BY AN
EXCLAMATION POINT. THE FRENCH
AND GERMAN VERSIONS AREN'T.
NEITHER IS THE ENGLISH VERSION.
I WONDER IF THIS IS SOME KIND
OF CULTURAL STEREOTYPING. AS
IF THE ONLY WAY TO GET AN IT-
ALIAN TO PAY ATTENTION TO SOME-
THING IS TO YELL AT THEM, OR
MAKE A CRAZY HAND GESTURE. THE
INDICATIVE IS OKAY FOR EVERY-
ONE ELSE, BUT THE IMPERATIVE

IS RESERVED FOR ITALIANS. I
ASK SERGIO IF HE THINKS THIS
IS OFFENSIVE. HE SHRUGS.
"NO, IT'S TRUE."

DEAR SCANDINAVIAN LADY AT THE
CAFE IN NAPLES —
SORRY. THIS ISN'T A VERY
FLATTERING PORTRAIT OF YOU.

"CONTROLLED SUBSTANCES, OBSCENE ARTICLES, AND TOXIC SUBSTANCES ARE GENERALLY PROHIBITED ENTRY. THANK YOU, AND WELCOME TO THE UNITED STATES. "

AS MUCH AS I HATE BORDER COPS, I LIKE BORDER FORMALITIES. THE INK STAMPS AND THE DECLARATIONS. AT THE BORDER, YOU'RE NO LONGER JUST SOME ORDINARY PERSON. YOU'RE A SET OF HISTORICAL CIRCUMSTANCES AND GEOGRAPHICAL FACTS AND DIPLOMATIC RELATIONSHIPS. FOR A SECOND OR TWO, YOU ARE THE COUNTRY YOU'RE FROM, FOR BETTER OR FOR WORSE. BUT TODAY, FOR THE FIRST TIME IN A COUPLE MONTHS, MY PASSPORT MATCHES THE COUNTRY I'M

COMING INTO. "CITIZENSHIP?," THE
BORDER COP ASKS. "AMERICAN,"
I SAY. "UNFORTUNATELY" I WANT
TO ADD, BUT I DON'T. I DON'T
MENTION THAT I FEEL MORE LIKE
A DUAL CITIZEN : AMERICAN BY
BIRTH, BUT UNAMERICAN BY
INCLINATION.

AT THE PORT AUTHORITY BUS STATION,
I ASK THE GUY IN THE INFO
BOOTH IF THERE ARE ANY LUGGAGE
LOCKERS IN THE PLACE. "NOPE,"
HE SAYS. "THERE AREN'T ANY
LOCKERS IN THE WHOLE CITY
BECAUSE OF WHAT HAPPENED AT
THE WORLD TRADE CENTER."
THE INFO BOOTH GUY SAYS THIS
IN A WAY THAT SUGGESTS IT'S
PEOPLE LIKE ME WHO WANT TO
STASH THEIR BACKPACKS IN A
LOCKER WHO ARE AIDING AND

ABETTING THE TERRORISTS. I NOD AT THE INFO BOOTH GUY AND WALK AWAY, DAZZLED BY THE POSSIBILITIES OF THIS EXCUSE FOR ALL SORTS OF NEW YORK ANNOYANCES. CAN'T FIND A PARKING SPACE? OR A PUBLIC RESTROOM? OR A WORKING PAYPHONE? BLAME THE TERRORISTS.

DOWN IN THE SUBWAY, I WAIT FOR THE SEVENTH AVE. EXPRESS. WHEN THE TRAIN COMES, IT'S SUPER-COOLED, THE WAY THE TRAINS ARE DURING THE SUMMER. AFTER THE SWEATY CRUSH OF THE CROWDS, AND THE STINK OF PISS AND ROTTING GARBAGE ON THE PLATFORM, THERE'S SUDDENLY THE COOL SANCTUARY OF THE EXPRESS TRAIN. LIKE EVERY OTHER MOMENT OF SWEETNESS

IN THIS CITY, IT COMES UNEXPECT-
EDLY. WHICH IS HOW THIS
SICKO CITY MAKES YOU FALL IN
LOVE WITH IT. IT TREATS YOU
BAD AND STEALS YOUR CASH AND
MAKES YOU CRY, AND JUST WHEN
YOU THINK YOU'VE HAD ENOUGH,
AND YOU'RE GOING TO PACK YOUR
BAGS AND GO, THE CITY TURNS
ALL SOFT AND SWEET AND BEGS
YOU TO GIVE IT ANOTHER CHANCE.
AND OF COURSE, SUCKER THAT
YOU ARE, YOU DO.

I GET OFF THE TRAIN AT 116TH ST.
AND WALK A COUPLE BLOCKS TO
MY FAVORITE BAGEL PLACE,
WHERE I GET A SESAME BAGEL,
TOASTED, WITH TOFU CREAM
CHEESE — A HUGE GLOB OF THE
STUFF, MOST OF WHICH I SCRAPE
OFF. "IT'S A BAGEL THAT

TASTES LIKE A LUXURY BUT IS PRICED LIKE A STAPLE," I SAY TO MYSELF, REHEARSING FOR THE DAY I PRESENT MY REVOLUTIONARY THEORIES TO A DISTINGUISHED AUDIENCE OF SOCIAL SCIENTISTS. THEN I SIT DOWN AT A TABLE AND READ THE PAPER. THERE'S A STORY ABOUT THE SAXOPHONIST CANNONBALL ADDERLEY, HOW HE CAME TO NEW YORK IN THE 1950'S JUST TO SEE WHAT WAS GOING ON, AND NEXT THING YOU KNOW, HE OWNS THE PLACE. BACK THEN, THE RUSSIANS HAD A MILLION NUCLEAR MISSILES POINTED AT THE CITY, AND A LUGGAGE LOCKER AT THE PORT AUTHORITY BUS STATION COST A DIME.

TUCSON

IT'S NOT SO COLD THAT YOU
NEED THREE LAYERS OF SOCKS,
BUT IT'S COLD ENOUGH FOR A
HOODIE WITH THE HOOD UP.
THE ONLY THING I KNOW ABOUT
TUCSON ARE THE HOT MONTHS,
SO I BARELY RECOGNIZE THE
PLACE IN DECEMBER, WHEN
THE SWAMP COOLERS ARE SHUT
DOWN AND DRAINED AND
COVERED WITH BLUE TARPS. I
DRIVE TO TUCSON BY WAY OF
PHOENIX, WHICH EVERYBODY IN
TUCSON WILL TELL YOU IS A
BAD IDEA. PEOPLE IN TUCSON
HATE PHOENIX, BUT I'VE HAD
A SOFT SPOT FOR THE PLACE
EVER SINCE I FOUND A
RESTAURANT THAT SERVES

VEGAN SHRIMP PUFFS. IT'S CALLED
VEGGIE FUN. IT'S IN A LOW RENT
STRIP MALL NEAR A TANNING
SALON CALLED FUN TAN. THE
GUY WHO RUNS VEGGIE FUN IS
AN OLD ASIAN MAN WHOSE JET
BLACK HAIR MAY OR MAY NOT
BE REAL, AND WHO, FOR
REASONS THAT AREN'T CLEAR,
HAS CREATED A MENU THAT
INCLUDES VEGGIE FILET OF SOLE,
AND VEGGIE MUTTON WITH RICE,
AND VEGAN SHRIMP PUFFS —
LITTLE BALLS OF DEEP—FRIED
DOUGH FILLED WITH PINK TOFU
CREAM CHEESE. AFTER YOU EAT,
THE GUY GIVES YOU A COMPLI—
MENTARY CUP OF VEGAN VANILLA
SOFT-SERVE ICE CREAM. THAT'S

WHEN I FIND MYSELF FALLING IN
LOVE WITH PHOENIX — FREEWAYS
AND STRIP MALLS AND GOLF
COURSES AND ALL — AND FEELING
GRUMPY ABOUT TUCSON, WHERE
NO ONE EVER OFFERS YOU A
COMPLIMENTARY CUP OF ANYTHING.
WHILE I EAT MY ICE CREAM,
I THINK ABOUT HAPPINESS.
HOW IT'S ALWAYS TEMPORARY
AND UNPREDICTABLE, AND HOW
MOST OF THE TIME, YOU DON'T
EVEN RECOGNIZE IT TILL LATER,
WHEN YOU'RE FAR AWAY FROM
IT. SADNESS STICKS AROUND.
IT'S LIKE YOUR MOST RELIABLE
FRIEND. YOU CAN BE YOURSELF
AROUND SADNESS. IT'LL DRIVE
ACROSS COUNTRY WITH YOU AND
IT WON'T COMPLAIN IF THE FOOD

IS BAD OR THE MOTEL HAS
ROACHES. BUT HAPPINESS IS A
DIFFERENT STORY. IT'S ALWAYS
DITCHING YOU. LEAVING YOU
STUCK WITH THE BILL. THERE'S
NO ONE YOU'D RATHER SPEND YOUR
TIME WITH, AND HAPPINESS
KNOWS IT.

WHEN I GET TO TUCSON, I DECIDE
TO STAY AT THE HOTEL CONGRESS
BECAUSE I DON'T WANT TO BE
A MOOCH. I'M WORRIED THAT
MY FRIENDS ARE STARTING TO
THINK I ONLY VISIT THEM BE-
CAUSE THEY HAVE A COUCH I
CAN SLEEP ON. AND WHILE THIS
ISN'T TRUE — AFTER ALL, I
WOULDN'T SLEEP ON A COUCH
THAT BELONGS TO SOMEONE I
DON'T LIKE — I CAN'T DENY

THAT A COUCH IS PART OF MY
OVERALL VISITING CALCULUS.
WHICH MAKES ME A MOOCH. I
HATE MOOCHES. WHEN I HEAR
A STORY ABOUT A MOOCH, I
ALWAYS LIKE THE PART WHERE
SOMEONE FINALLY SAYS TO THE
MOOCH "HEY, GET A JOB!" SO
I GET A ROOM AT THE HOTEL
CONGRESS. THE ONE ADVANTAGE
OF THIS IS THAT I WON'T HAVE
TO DEAL WITH SARAH'S CAT. I'M
SCARED OF THAT CAT. IT HISSES
AT ME, AND WHEN I'M LYING
ON SARAH'S COUCH, IT STARES
AT ME UNPLEASANTLY. "I CAN
SEE RIGHT THROUGH YOU," THE
CAT SEEMS TO BE THINKING.
"YOU MOOCH." OF COURSE, IT
TAKES A LOT OF NERVE FOR A

PET CAT TO BE CALLING
ANYONE A MOOCH, BUT THAT'S
BESIDE THE POINT.

ONE NIGHT, SARAH COMES BY THE
HOTEL. WE SIT IN THE LOBBY,
AND I ASK HER IF SHE KNOWS
ABOUT ROOM 242. "I'VE HEARD
IT'S HAUNTED," I TELL HER.
SARAH SAYS WE SHOULD ASK
AL ABOUT THIS. AL WORKS AT
THE FRONT DESK. HE SAYS,
YES, HE KNOWS ABOUT ROOM 242
AND IT'S GOT NOTHING TO DO
WITH GHOSTS. THERE USED TO
BE A LONG-TERM RESIDENT WHO
LIVED IN THAT ROOM, AN
OLDER LADY WHO WAS ALWAYS
A LITTLE NUTTY. AS TIME
PASSED, SHE GOT CRAZIER. ONE

FRIDAY NIGHT, WHILE THE HOTEL
WAS REALLY BUSY, SHE FLIPPED
OUT. SHE CALLED THE COPS AND
SAID SOMEONE WAS TRYING TO
KILL HER. SHE ALSO HAD A GUN,
AND AT SOME POINT, SHE TOOK
A POTSHOT OUT HER WINDOW.
NEXT THING YOU KNOW, THE
COPS EVACUATED THE HOTEL
AND BLOCKADED THE STREET.
THEN THEY YELLED AT THE LADY
THROUGH A BULLHORN, TELLING
HER IF SHE DIDN'T SURRENDER,
THEY'D FIRE A CANNISTER OF
TEAR GAS INTO HER ROOM. THE
LADY YELLED AT THE COPS THAT
IF THEY DID THAT, SHE'D SHOOT
HERSELF IN THE HEAD. THE
COPS FIRED THE TEAR GAS. THE
LADY SHOT HERSELF. AL SAYS

SOME PEOPLE SAY THE ROOM IS
HAUNTED, BUT THAT JUST MAKES
HIM MAD — THAT PEOPLE WANT
A GHOST STORY INSTEAD OF
THE REAL STORY.

IN THE MORNING, I CHECK OUT
OF THE HOTEL CONGRESS BECAUSE
I CAN'T AFFORD NOT TO BE A
MOOCH ANYMORE. THEN I MEET
UP WITH SARAH AND LINDSEY
AND WE GET TACOS AT THE
LITTLE TACQUERIA WHERE SARAH
USED TO WORK. HER OLD BOSS
IS A BAD MAN — OR MAYBE A
GOOD MAN WHOSE BAD SIDE GETS
THE BETTER OF HIM — AND IN
THE END, HE FIRED HER. BUT
THIS BAD MAN MAKES REALLY
GOOD VEGGIE TACOS. THEY'RE
FILLED WITH VEGGIE CHORIZO
AND GRILLED PEPPERS, AND

THEY'RE WRAPPED IN HOMEMADE CORN TORTILLAS. AT FIRST, RIGHT AFTER SHE WAS FIRED, SARAH WOULD ASK LINDSEY TO BUY TACOS FOR HER SO SHE WOULDN'T HAVE TO GO INSIDE THE PLACE. BUT PRETTY SOON, SARAH STARTED EATING AT THE RESTAURANT AGAIN. I THINK THIS TORTURED HER FOR A WHILE. LIKE HER APPETITES WERE MORE POWERFUL THAN HER PRINCIPLES. BUT THEN SHE DECIDED THAT A GOOD CHEAP TACO IS A PRINCIPLE ALL ITS OWN, AND SHE STOPPED WORRYING ABOUT IT.

GERMANY: SOFA IMPRISONS MAN A man was trapped for hours in his folding sofa bed after it sprang shut on him when he tried to get something out of it, the police in the southwestern town of Kenzingen said. "Unfortunately, he was so stuck that he couldn't move," a police spokesman said. After several hours of knocking and shouting, the man was finally heard by neighbors, who called the police and an ambulance.

BIOSPHERE 2

BIOSPHERE 2 IS A RICH GUY'S
SCIENCE FAIR PROJECT. THAT'S
HOW SARAH PUTS IT. BACK IN
THE 1980's, A TEXAS OIL
BILLIONAIRE NAMED ED BASS
DECIDED TO BUILD A HUGE,
TOTALLY SEALED TERRARIUM IN
THE DESERT NORTH OF TUCSON.
WHY AN OIL TYCOON DECIDED TO
BUILD A GIANT, HIGH TECH
GREENHOUSE ISN'T ENTIRELY
CLEAR, BUT IT SEEMS TO HAVE
INVOLVED A SHADY ECO-CULT
CALLED THE INSTITUTE FOR
ECOTECHNICS; A COLLECTION OF
HIPPY SCIENTISTS; WILLIAM S.
BURROUGHS; AND A PLAN TO
COLONIZE MARS. BIOSPHERE 2

WAS SUPPOSED TO BE A MINIATURE
VERSION OF EARTH (AKA,
BIOSPHERE 1). MINIATURE AND,
APPARENTLY, PORTABLE. A LABORA-
TORY FOR LIVING OFF-WORLD. BY
1990, IT WAS FINISHED: A GIANT
GLASS-AND-STEEL MAYAN-REVIVAL
SCI-FI GREENHOUSE WITH ITS OWN
COMPUTER-CONTROLLED RAINFOREST,
A COUPLE TYPES OF DESERT, SOME
MONKEYS AND PIGS, AND A MILLION
GALLON SALTWATER OCEAN
EQUIPPED WITH A WAVE MACHINE.
FROM THE BEGINNING, TOURISTS
WERE INVITED TO VISIT, WHICH
MADE BIOSPHERE 2 LESS AN ECO-
LOGICAL LABORATORY THAN AN
ECOLOGICAL-LABORATORY-THEMED
ROADSIDE ATTRACTION.

SARAH AND I VISIT B2 ON A TUESDAY

IN EARLY DECEMBER. SARAH IS A TEACHER, AND SHE WANTS TO DO A FIELD TRIP FACTFINDING MISSION. THE TOUR GROUP CONSISTS OF SARAH AND ME, TWO RETIRED COUPLES, AND A TOUR GUIDE NAMED LYNN. LYNN TELLS US THAT ORIGINALLY, THE IDEA WAS TO LOCK A BUNCH OF SCIENTISTS (WELL, NOT SCIENTISTS, EXACTLY, BUT PEOPLE WITH "SCIENTIFIC BACKGROUNDS ") IN THE BIOSPHERE AND SEE IF THEY COULD SURVIVE FOR A COUPLE YEARS. EIGHT BIOSPHERIANS EVENTUALLY TOOK THE PLUNGE. AT FIRST, THINGS WENT WELL. THERE WERE TONS OF TOURISTS. THE FRUIT TREES IN THE RAINFOREST PRODUCED FRUIT. THE

CHICKENS LAID EGGS. BUT THEN
THINGS BEGAN TO GO WRONG. THE
PIGS STARTED TO RAID THE VEGE-
TABLE GARDENS. THE MONKEYS
SHRIEKED ALL NIGHT AND MADE IT
HARD FOR THE BIOSPHERIANS TO
SLEEP. THE BEES DIED. BUT THESE
WERE MINOR DIFFICULTIES. THE
REAL TROUBLE BEGAN WHEN THE
OXYGEN LEVELS INSIDE THE BIO-
SPHERE BEGAN TO PLUMMET. NO
ONE COULD FIGURE OUT WHY.
THANKS TO THE LACK OF OXYGEN,
THE BIOSPHERIANS BEGAN TO
STUMBLE AROUND AND BUMP INTO
WALLS. THINGS WERE GETTING
OUT OF CONTROL. I FIND OUT LATER
THAT THE BIOSPHERIANS SPLIT
INTO TWO FACTIONS: THE TRUE
BELIEVERS WHO WOULD DO ANY-
THING TO MAKE THE PROJECT

WORK, AND THE REALISTS WHO THOUGHT IT WOULDN'T BE A BAD IDEA TO OPEN A WINDOW AND LET IN SOME FRESH AIR. IN THE END, MISSION CONTROL DECIDED TO PUMP IN SOME OXYGEN. THEY DIDN'T REALLY HAVE A CHOICE, BUT IT PRETTY MUCH DEFEATED THE WHOLE "SEALED, SELF-CONTAINED ENVIRONMENT" THING. TWO YEARS LATER, WHEN THE BIO-SPHERIANS FINALLY EMERGED FROM THE BIOSPHERE, THEY WERE PALE (SINCE THE GREENHOUSE GLASS FILTERED OUT UV LIGHT), AND SKINNY (SINCE THE VARIOUS ECOSYSTEMS BARELY PRODUCED ENOUGH FOOD), AND PRETTY SICK OF BIOSPHERE 2.

LYNN TAKES US INSIDE. ORIGINALLY,
THE GREENHOUSE WAS SEALED UP
AND TOURISTS COULDN'T GO INSIDE.
NOW IT DOESN'T MATTER. WE
WALK THROUGH THE B2 GOURMET
KITCHEN, AND PAST A B2
BEDROOM THAT'S GOT ABSTRACT
EXPRESSIONIST PAINTINGS HANGING
ON THE WALLS. ONE OF THE
BIOSPHERIANS PAINTED THEM,
APPARENTLY WHILE SUFFERING
FROM ACUTE OXYGEN DEPRIVATION.
WE TROOP THROUGH THE RAIN-
FOREST, AND STARE AT THE
MILLION GALLON OCEAN. THE
LONELY THROB OF THE WAVE
MACHINE, SLOW AND REGULAR, IS
LIKE THE FADING PULSE OF SOME
MONSTROUS DYING THING. WE
STAND THERE, LOOKING OUT OVER

A DEAD SEA UNDER A HAZY GLASS SKY. LYNN TELLS US THERE WASN'T ENOUGH MONEY TO CONSTRUCT A SOLAR POWER SYSTEM AND MAKE B2 TRULY SELF-SUFFICIENT. INSTEAD, IT GETS ITS ELECTRICITY OFF THE LOCAL GRID. NO ONE ON THE TOUR SAYS IT, BUT I GET THE FEELING WE'RE ALL COMING TO THE SAME CONCLUSION: THAT BIOSPHERE 2 ISN'T JUST A FAILURE, BUT A COLOSSAL FIASCO. THIS THOUGHT CAUSES ALL OF US TO LAPSE INTO A KIND OF EMBARRASSED SILENCE.

AFTER THE TOUR, LYNN DITCHES US, LEAVING US ALL TO WANDER AROUND THE PLACE ALONE AND UNSUPERVISED. THERE ARE NO SURVEILLANCE CAMERAS. NO

DOCENTS OR SECURITY GUARDS. I
TELL SARAH I FEEL LIKE WE'RE
ASTRONAUTS WHO'VE RESPONDED
TO A DISTRESS CALL FROM A
DISTANT SPACE STATION. WHEN
WE GET THERE, THE MACHINES ARE
RUNNING AND THE COMPUTERS
ARE AUTOMATICALLY TAKING CARE
OF THINGS, BUT THE SPACE STATION
CREW HAS VANISHED WITHOUT A
TRACE. "YEAH, LIKE ALIEN,"
SARAH SAYS. "OR WRATH OF KHAN,"
I SAY. WE WANDER DOWN INTO
THE BASEMENT, A CONCRETE
BUNKER FULL OF JILLION-GALLON
WATER TANKS AND EVAPORATIVE
COOLERS AS BIG AS TRUCKS. THE
MACHINES WORKED JUST FINE.
DROPPING PRECISELY THE RIGHT
AMOUNT OF RAIN ON THE SIMULATED
RAINFOREST. DE-HUMIDIFYING THE

SIMULATED DESERT. THE MACHINERY WAS JUST ABOUT THE ONLY THING THAT WORKED ACCORDING TO PLAN.

BY 1994, THINGS GOT UGLY. ED BASS WANTED TO CAN THE HIPPY VISIONARIES MANAGING B2. THE MANAGERS REFUSED TO GO. RESTRAINING ORDERS WERE ISSUED. FEDERAL MARSHALS SHOWED UP. AT SOME POINT— AND THIS IS WHERE THINGS GET ESPECIALLY MURKY— A COUPLE FORMER BIOSPHERIANS (ONE OF WHOM WAS A BELGIAN ENGINEER WHO CALLED HIMSELF LASER) ALLEGEDLY BROKE INTO BIOSPHERE IN THE DEAD OF NIGHT AND OPENED ALL THE EMERGENCY EXITS AND BUSTED A FEW WINDOWS. I'M NOT SURE WHY THEY DID THIS.

NEEDLESS TO SAY, THE BILLIONAIRE
OIL TYCOON AND THE ECO-MYSTICS
WERE NO LONGER ON SPEAKING
TERMS. BASS FINALLY MANAGED TO
GET RID OF THEM, AND CONVINCED
COLUMBIA UNIVERSITY TO TAKE
OVER MANAGEMENT OF THE PLACE.
COLUMBIA TRIED TO MOVE AWAY
FROM THE DISNEY SCIENCE OF
THE ORIGINAL BIOSPHERE 2 AND
DO SOME REAL ENVIRONMENTAL
RESEARCH. BUT COLUMBIA RE-
CENTLY BAILED OUT, AND NOW
B2'S FUTURE IS UP FOR GRABS.
THERE ARE RUMORS THAT ED
BASS WANTS TO DEVELOP THE LAND.
BUILD A BUNCH OF TRACT HOMES.
MAYBE CALL IT BIOSPHERE
ESTATES.
ON THE WAY BACK TO THE CAR,
SARAH AND I WALK PAST A ROW

OF INTERPRETIVE PLAQUES THAT NEITHER OF US READS. WE'RE PRETTY SURE WE KNOW WHAT THEY DON'T SAY. THAT BIOSPHERE 2 HAS ALL THE ELEMENTS OF A GREEK TRAGEDY. A NOT VERY GOOD, B-GRADE GREEK TRAGEDY, FEATURING A HUBRISTIC TEXAS BILLIONAIRE, A CHORUS OF WEIRDO SCIENTISTS, AN INSANE SCHEME, AND A SERIES OF DISASTERS THAT REDUCES THE WHOLE THING TO A SHAMBLES. MAYBE — JUST MAYBE — THAT WAS THE PLAN ALL ALONG. MAYBE ED BASS IS AN ECO-RADICAL GENIUS, AND HE RIGHTLY CALCULATED THAT THE BEST WAY TO DEMONSTRATE THE FRAGILITY OF BIOSPHERE 1 WAS TO BUILD BIOSPHERE 2 AND WATCH IT CRASH AND BURN. A

DRAMATIC LESSON THAT MIGHT
CAUSE PEOPLE TO SET ASIDE
THEIR PLANS TO COLONIZE MARS,
AND TO STOP TREATING THIS
PLANET LIKE A DISPOSIBLE
DIAPER. IF THAT WAS THE
PLAN, THEN IT DIDN'T WORK,
EITHER.

TUCSON.

Tucson

NINETEEN BUCKS WILL BUY YOU A
MOTEL ROOM ON THE MIRACLE
MILE. YOU'LL GET A DOOR WITH
A DENT WHERE SOMEONE — A
COP, OR A PIMP, OR THE GUY YOU
JUST SOLD BAD WEED TO — TRIED
TO KICK IT IN. YOU'LL GET A
TV WITH DIRTY MOVIES AND NO
HORIZONTAL HOLD. THE BED WILL
BE A BEAT-DOWN THING SLUMPED
IN THE MIDDLE OF THE ROOM,
BARELY ABLE TO HOLD ITSELF UP.
IT'LL HAVE ELABORATELY STAINED
SHEETS. SHOE POLISH. BLOOD.
LIPSTICK AND CIGARETTE BURNS.
SHEETS THAT ARE MORE LIKE ART
THAN LAUNDRY; MARKED BY THE
ACCIDENTAL EXPRESSIONISM OF ALL
THOSE BODIES THAT HAVE BEEN

TANGLED UP IN THEM. ON THE MIRACLE MILE, THERE'S A MOTEL CALLED THE GHOST RANCH, AND A MOTEL WITH A METH LAB IN A NON-SMOKING ROOM, AND A MOTEL WITH A GUARD DOG THAT'LL TRY TO KILL YOU WHEN YOU DROP OFF YOUR KEY AT THE FRONT DESK. THE MOTELS ON THE MIRACLE MILE AREN'T LISTED IN THE KIND OF GUIDE BOOKS THAT RESPECTABLE TOURISTS READ. THEY DON'T BELONG TO THE BETTER BUSINESS BUREAU, OR OFFER A AAA DISCOUNT. THE PEOPLE WHO STAY AT THESE MOTELS AREN'T NECESSARILY LOOKING FOR A GOOD NIGHT'S SLEEP. SOME OF THEM ARE JUST LOOKING FOR A PLACE TO SPEND THE NIGHT, WIDE AWAKE.

Moriarty

THE GREYHOUND STATION IN MORIARTY, NEW MEXICO IS A DUSTY PARKING LOT OFF THE FREEWAY ACCESS ROAD. THERE'S A TEENAGED GIRL WAITING FOR THE BUS ALONG WITH HER MOM AND A COUPLE GUYS. THE MOM IS WEARING TIGHTS AND PLATFORM SHOES, AND HER FACE IS WRINKLED FROM TOO MUCH SUN. THE TWO GUYS ARE WEARING PUFFY SKI PARKAS. ONE OF THEM IS STUBBLY AND THE OTHER ONE HAS A BIG SHAGGY BEARD. THEY LOOK LIKE THE KIND OF GUYS YOU WOULDN'T WANT TO FIND FOLLOWING YOU OUT OF A BAR. THE TEENAGED GIRL IS HOLDING A BOUQUET OF FLOWERS. SHE HUGS HER MOM AND CLIMBS

ONTO THE BUS. HER MOM AND THE
TWO GUYS GET INTO A LONG
GREEN 1970's CHEVY AND DRIVE
AWAY. THE GIRL SITS DOWN
ACROSS THE AISLE FROM A
SKETCHY GUY WITH COWBOY BOOTS
AND A MULLET WHO GOT ON THE
BUS IN ALBUQUERQUE. THEY
START CHATTING. THE GIRL'S NAME
IS ELENA. SHE'S FROM MORIARTY,
"BUT EVERYONE HERE CALLS IT
MORTUARY." THE MULLET GUY
ASKS HER WHO THOSE PEOPLE
WERE WHO DROPPED HER OFF.
ELENA SAYS IT WAS HER MOM
AND HER BROTHER AND SOME DUDE
WHO WAS TRYING TO HOOK UP WITH
HER. "THAT DUDE LOOKED KIND OF
SPUN," THE MULLET GUY LAUGHS.
"WHICH ONE?" ELENA ASKS.
"THE DUDE WITH THE BEARD, "

THE MULLET GUY SAYS. "THAT'S MY BROTHER," ELENA SAYS. THE MULLET GUY CLEARS HIS THROAT. "OH, YEAH?" HE SAYS. "YEAH," ELENA SAYS.

THE BUS HEADS EAST ON I-40, THEN CUTS DOWN TO CLOVIS ON HIGHWAY 84. OUTSIDE, IT'S THE EARLIEST KIND OF SPRING, THE TIME OF YEAR IN WEST TEXAS WHEN ONE MINUTE YOU'RE IN SHORTS, AND THE NEXT MINUTE IT'S SNOWING. OUTSIDE, EVERY-THING THAT'S NOT A ROAD OR A FARM HOUSE OR A TOWN & COUNTRY CONVENIENCE STORE IS A COTTON FIELD. IT WASN'T ALWAYS LIKE THIS. THE HIGH PLAINS USED TO BE A NO-MAN'S-LAND. AN EMPTY QUARTER THAT ONLY

COMMANCHE INAIANS AND CATTLE RUSTLERS DARED TO CROSS. THEN THE FARMERS CAME AND CUT THE SOD. THESE DAYS, COTTON FARMERS PLOW THE FIELDS THE WAY AN ACCOUNTANT GOES OVER THE BOOKS. LINE AFTER LINE. ROW AFTER ROW. MAKING THE LANDSCAPE OVER INTO A LEDGER SHEET. IT'S NOT THE WILDERNESS ANYMORE, EXCEPT ON WINDY DAYS IN MARCH WHEN THE DUST BLOWS. THAT'S WHEN THE WORLD TURNS THE COLOR OF DIRT, AND COTTON FARMERS IN PICK-UP TRUCKS KEEP SWERVING OUT OF THE WAY OF ON-COMING TUMBLEWEEDS. THE WIND IN MARCH IS A TROUBLEMAKER. IT INCITES THE COTTON FIELDS TO RIOT.

"REMEMBER HOW IT USED TO BE?" THE WIND'LL SAY. "WHEN YOU WERE YOUNG AND WILD? NOW LOOK AT YOU. CROPS? I NEVER THOUGHT I'D SEE THE DAY WHEN WILD WEST TEXAS WOULD TURN INTO A COTTON PATCH!" THAT'S ALL IT TAKES TO GET THOSE FIELDS WHOOPIN' IT UP AND FILLING THE AIR FULL OF DUST. TOMORROW, THE COTTON FIELDS WILL HAVE A HANGOVER, BUT TODAY THEY'RE ON A DRUNK.

RATON, NM.
AMTRAK STATION

LUBBOCK

I SPEND A YEAR LIKE A HOBO,
CATCHING RIDES ON COUCHES
INSTEAD OF BOXCARS. LAST
NIGHT, I GOT BACK TO TEXAS, AND
I STRETCHED OUT ON MY OLD BED
IN MY OLD HOMETOWN AND FELL
ASLEEP. A FAMILIAR SLEEP. LIKE
IT'D BEEN WAITING FOR ME HERE
THE WHOLE TIME I WAS AWAY,
CURLED UP IN THE CORNER OF
MY ROOM. IN THE MORNING, IT'S
SNOWING, AND BY THE TIME THE
SUN SETS, THE SNOW IS PRETTY
DEEP. I TAKE A LONG WALK,
THINKING OVER THE LAST YEAR
AND WHAT I'D DONE WITH IT.
THE MOON IS OUT, A FULL MOON
REFLECTED BY EVERY SNOW
FLAKE ON THE GROUND. LIKE IT'D

SNOWED FULL MOONS INSTEAD OF
SNOWFLAKES. I TRY TO CONVINCE
MYSELF THAT I'M NOT SOME GOOD-
FOR-NOTHING NOMAD, BUT THAT I'M
A SCIENTIST, AND I'VE BEEN
CONDUCTING IMPORTANT RESEARCH
ON THE CHAIRS PEOPLE SIT IN
WHEN THEY'RE WAITING FOR SOME-
THING : A TRAIN, OR A BUS, OR A
FERRY THAT WILL FLOAT THEM
FROM THE DISAPPOINTMENTS ON THIS
SHORE TO THE HAPPY LIFE WAITING
ON THE OTHER SIDE. CHAIRS
DESIGNED NOT TO LET YOU SLEEP,
BUT THAT PROP YOU UP WITH METAL
PIPING AND VINYL STRAPS,
PILLORYING YOU LIKE A WAYWARD
PURITAN. I'VE DONE FIELD RE-
SEARCH IN ROOMS FULL OF CHAIRS
LIKE THESE, WHERE YOU SIT AND
FEEL TIME PRESS DOWN ON YOU,

THE WAY NOSEDIVING FIGHTER
PILOTS EXPERIENCE MAXIMUM
G'S. AND I'VE WORKED OUT THE
DETAILS OF A WHOLE NEW
FIELD: TRAVEL ANESTHESIOLOGY.
YOU ARRIVE AT A BUS STATION
OR AN AIRPORT, AND A
SPECIALLY-TRAINED TICKET
AGENT CHECKS YOUR LUGGAGE
AND STICKS AN I.V. NEEDLE IN
YOUR ARM. THEN YOU'RE CON-
VEYED UNCONSCIOUS TO YOUR
DESTINATION, WHERE A
SPECIALLY-TRAINED TAXI DRIVER
REVIVES YOU AND ASKS "WHERE
YA HEADED, MACK?" BUT
TONIGHT, I'M HAVING SECOND
THOUGHTS ABOUT TRAVEL ANES-
THESIOLOGY. MAYBE IT'S A BAD
IDEA TO TREAT WAITING LIKE AN
AILMENT. OR TIME LIKE A

TREATABLE CONDITION. BECAUSE,
OF COURSE, THERE IS NO
TREATMENT, AND THERE IS
NO CURE.

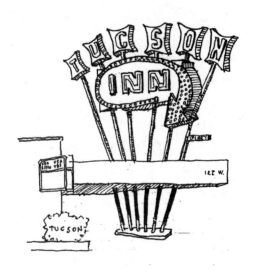

LUBBOCK

MY PARENTS' PLUMBER IS A STONER.
HIS NAME IS PHIL. AT LEAST,
HE USED TO BE A STONER BACK
IN THE 70'S. HE TELLS ME HE
HAD HAIR DOWN TO HIS BUTT
AND HE RODE AROUND ON A
HARLEY, BUT NOW HE'S RESPECT-
ABLE, MORE OR LESS. I LIKE
PHIL. HE'S A CLOSET FREAK,
WHICH IS WHAT YOU HAVE TO BE
WHEN YOU'RE A PLUMBER IN
WEST TEXAS. NO ONE WOULD
HIRE HIM TO FIX THEIR LEAKS
OR UNCLOG THEIR DRAINS IF
THEY KNEW HE USED TO BE A
POTHEAD. I ASK PHIL HOW HE
CAN STAND LIVING IN LUBBOCK,
A TOWN WHERE THE CHURCHES
AND THE S.U.V.'S JUST KEEP
GETTING BIGGER, AND THE POLITICS

JUST KEEP GETTING WORSE. HE
TELLS ME THAT WHEN YOU'RE A
PLUMBER, YOU SEE WHAT'S IN
PEOPLE'S BASEMENTS AND
ATTICS AND WHAT'S UNDER THEIR
SINKS, AND HE SAYS THAT
PEOPLE'S LIVES ARE JUST AS
MESSY HERE AS THEY ARE ANY-
WHERE ELSE. PHIL TELLS ME
ABOUT A HOUSE HE WORKED ON
NOT FAR FROM WHERE MY PAR-
ENTS LIVE. MY PARENTS' NEIGH-
BORHOOD — THE NEIGHBORHOOD
WHERE I GREW UP — IS PRETTY
STRAITLACED, EVEN BY LUBBOCK
STANDARDS, WHICH PROBABLY
MAKES IT ONE OF THE MOST
STRAITLACED NEIGHBORHOODS ON
THE PLANET EARTH. PHIL GOT
CALLED OUT TO THIS HOUSE
BECAUSE THE AIR CONDITIONER

WAS ON THE BLINK. PHIL FIXES
AIR CONDITIONERS, TOO. WHEN
HE GOT THERE, THE OWNER WAS
ACTING STRANGE. HE TOLD PHIL
THE A/C IS IN THE BASEMENT.
THEN HE PAUSED. "HAVE YOU EVER
SMOKED POT?" HE ASKED. PHIL
FIGURED THIS GUY HAD SOMEHOW
DISCOVERED HIS SECRET PAST
LIFE, SO HE DECIDED TO BE
HONEST. "YEAH," PHIL SAID,
"I SMOKED A LOT OF POT. BUT
NOW I'M A LICENSED PLUMBER
AND I'M TOTALLY CLEAN."
"WELL," THE GUY SAID, "IF YOU
SEE ANYTHING... UNUSUAL... IN
THE BASEMENT, I'D BE GRATE-
FUL IF YOU'D JUST IGNORE IT."
IT TURNED OUT THE BASEMENT
WAS FULL OF POT PLANTS.
DOZENS OF THEM. SITTING IN

LITTLE FLOWER POTS UNDERNEATH A BANK OF GLO-LAMPS. "SO LUBBOCK'S NOT SO BAD," PHIL SAYS, WHICH MAY NOT BE THE MORAL OF THIS STORY TO THE AVERAGE LUBBOCKITE, BUT THAT'S BECAUSE PHIL ISN'T.

PITTSBURGH

YOU THINK THE TRAIN IS LATE WHEN
IT'S AN HOUR LATE, TILL IT'S
SUDDENLY 5 HOURS LATE, AND
AN HOUR LATE SEEMS EARLY.
AMTRAK IS LIKE THAT. ALTERING
THE WAY YOU PERCEIVE TIME.
I WALK OVER TO THE BUS STATION
WHICH IS ACROSS THE STREET
FROM THE TRAIN STATION. THERE'S
AN ALL-NIGHT RESTAURANT OVER
THERE CALLED THE TRAVELER'S
CAFÉ. THE PLACE HAS AN
APPALACHIAN THEME. AT LEAST,
I THINK THAT'S THE THEME.
EXPOSED FAKE WOODEN BEAMS
AND A FAKE LOG CABIN. IT'S
ALSO DIMLY LIT, WHICH IS
WEIRD FOR A BUS STATION

DINER. USUALLY, THOSE PLACES
ARE LIT-UP LIKE A USED CAR
LOT; AS IF, WITH ENOUGH
WATTAGE, THEY CAN DRIVE OFF
THE NIGHT AND ALL THE BAD
STUFF THAT COMES WITH IT.
BUT THIS DINER IS DIM, IN A
WAY THAT'S PART-CREEPY AND
PART-SOMETHING ELSE. LIKE AN
ACT OF MERCY. LIKE IT'S OKAY
FOR YOU TO SLIDE INTO A RED
VINYL BOOTH NEXT TO A LITTLE
LOG CABIN AND CATCH A FEW Z'S
IN THE GLOOM.
I BUY A CUP OF COFFEE AT THE
COUNTER FROM A GUY WITH
PRISON TATTOOS ON THE BACK OF
HIS HANDS. HE'S SUPER POLITE.
MAYBE EVEN A LITTLE SYMPATHETIC.
LIKE HE KNOWS MY TRAIN IS

FIVE HOURS LATE AND I'M STUCK IN PITTSBURGH AT 3 IN THE MORNING, AND THIS CUP OF COFFEE IS A LITTLE FAVOR HE CAN DO FOR ME.

NEXT TIME I'M IN PITTSBURGH, THE SAME THING HAPPENS. MY TRAIN IS LATE, SO I HEAD OVER TO THE BUS STATION. ONLY THIS TIME, THE BUS STATION IS SHUT DOWN AND SURROUNDED BY A CHAIN LINK FENCE, AND THE TRAVELER'S CAFÉ IS GONE. THEY SEEM TO BE RENOVATING THE WHOLE PLACE. I HAVE ABSOLUTELY NO DOUBT THAT IN THE NEW BUS STATION THERE'LL BE A NEW DINER, AND IT'LL BE LIT-UP AS BRIGHT AS A USED CAR LOT.

THE RAVEN'S
GRIN INN
MT. CARROLL, IL.

THEFUCKENRADTOUROFTHEWORLD.

JIM WARFIELD RUNS A YEAR-ROUND
HAUNTED HOUSE. IT'S IN MT.
CARROLL, AT THE FAR WEST SIDE
OF ILLINOIS, IN THE MIDDLE OF
NOWHERE. DROP BY MOST ANY
NIGHT BETWEEN 7 AND MIDNIGHT
AND HE'LL GIVE YOU A TOUR. BUT
NO- IT'S MORE THAN A TOUR. IT'S
PERFORMANCE ART. AND ACTUALLY,
THE RAVEN'S GRIN INN IS MORE
THAN A HAUNTED HOUSE. IT'S
A FOLK ART MASTERPIECE.
I STOP BY LATE ONE NIGHT IN
EARLY JANUARY. MT. CARROLL IS

QUIET. REALLY QUIET.
THE INN IS ON A
DEAD END STREET
BEHIND CHARLIE'S
BAR. IT DOESN'T
LOOK LIKE ANYONE'S
AROUND. I RING THE BELL.

FARE
PER MILE

THERE'S AN OLD TAXI CAB DOOR
MOUNTED ON THE SIDE OF THE
HOUSE. THE WINDOW SLOWLY
ROLLS DOWN.
"YEEES?" JIM ASKS IN A SPOOKY
BARITONE.
"I'D LIKE A
TOUR PLEASE."
I PAY TEN BUCKS.
NEXT THING
I KNOW, JIM
COMES SAILING
DOWN HIS FRONT
DOOR / DRAWBRIDGE
DRESSED LIKE A
NAZI STORM TROOPER. HE INVITES
ME INSIDE.

COME THIS
WAY...

THE INN IS AS MUCH A FUN HOUSE AS A SPOOK HOUSE. FOR THE NEXT TWO HOURS, I WANDER THROUGH COCKEYED SECRET PASSAGES...

AND SLIDE DOWN SLIDES THAT WHISK ME FROM ONE FLOOR OF THE HOUSE TO THE NEXT.

(ACTUAL TERROR)

NO!!

THE BIG ATTRACTION, THOUGH, IS JIM. ONE MINUTE, HE'S MAKING PENIS PUNS, THE NEXT, HE'S GRABBING YOUR FINGER AND TELLING YOU THAT GHOSTLY VOICES ARE COMMANDING HIM TO LOP IT OFF WITH PRUNING SHEARS.

JIM BUILT EVERY-
THING IN THE HOUSE.
THE SPACE ALIEN
DIORAMA, THE
TALKING REFRIGER-
ATOR. HE DUG A
TUNNEL TO THE
BASEMENT, AND
HE ENGINEERED THE "BAD DREAM BED SLIDE."
YEAH, THE BED SLIDE. YOU LIE DOWN ON
A LITTLE MATTRESS ON THE FLOOR.
A SIGN BY YOUR HEAD TELLS YOU THAT
TWO PEOPLE HAVE BROKEN THEIR LEGS
ON THE THING. "IS THIS SAFE?" YOU
ASK JIM. "USUALLY," HE REPLIES.
HE WRAPS YOUR LEGS IN A BLACK
SHEET. HE STICKS YOUR ARMS IN
A PADDED SLEEVE.

"I CAN'T MOVE," YOU SAY TO JIM.
"PERFECT," JIM SAYS.

AT THE FOOT OF THE MATTRESS
IS A LITTLE DOOR IN THE WALL.
IT LOOKS LIKE A GARBAGE SHOOT.

"RELAX," JIM SAYS. "IT'S EASIER
THAT WAY."

LATER, AFTER MY
HEAD CLEARED,
THIS IS WHAT
I DETERMINED:
THAT THE
MATTRESS WENT
VERT; THAT IT
PITCHED ME IN
A GARBAGE
SHOOT; THAT I
FREE FELL

THROUGH UTTER DARKNESS FOR
SEVERAL VERY LONG SECONDS;
THAT, AT A BEND IN THE SHOOT,
I NEARLY SNAPPED MY SPINE;
THAT I LANDED IN A BATTERED,
BROKEN PILE IN THE PITCH-BLACK,
REPORTEDLY-HAUNTED SUBBASEMENT.
AS I LAY THERE, WRITHING IN
PAIN, I HAD THE SAME THOUGHT
THAT PROBABLY HUNDREDS OF
OTHER VISITORS HAVE HAD AT
THIS SAME MOMENT: JIM
WARFIELD, YOU'RE A GENIUS.

MICHIGAN

IF YOU HOLD UP YOUR RIGHT HAND
WITH THE PALM POINTED TOWARD
YOUR FACE, AND YOU SQUEEZE
YOUR FINGERS TOGETHER AND
LEAVE YOUR THUMB STICKING OUT—
THAT'S MICHIGAN. DETROIT IS
WHERE YOUR THUMB ATTACHES
TO THE REST OF YOUR HAND, AND
HIGHWAY 12 RUNS A LITTLE
NORTH OF BUT PARALLEL TO
THE PATH THE BLADE FOLLOWS
AS YOU SLIT YOUR WRIST. HIGH-
WAY 12 IS THE ROAD I TAKE FROM
CHICAGO TO DETROIT. IT RUNS
PAST A HYDROPONIC TOMATO FARM,
AND A FIBERGLASS FISH THAT
SPINS ON A POLE, AND A FLASHING
HIGHWAY SIGN THAT ASKS "IS

YOUR CAR WINTERIZED? " IT PASSES
THROUGH NEW BUFFALO, AND
THREE OAKS, AND MOTTVILLE,
WHERE I STOP TO TAKE A LOOK
AT A BRIDGE. A HISTORICAL
PLAQUE SAYS IT'S A CAMELBACK
BRIDGE, BUILT IN 1922. IT
GETS ITS NAME FROM THE THREE
CONCRETE HUMPS THAT HOLD
UP THE ROAD. I STAND ON THE
BRIDGE, AND THE AIR SMELLS
LIKE BURNING LEAVES. ALL
DAY, I'VE PASSED PILES OF
LEAVES, RAKED UP AND SET ON
FIRE. FUNERAL PYRES FOR
ANOTHER SEASON THAT'S DIED
AWAY. MOST OF THE PILES I'VE
PASSED JUST SMOLDER, SENDING
CLOUDS OF SMOKE INTO THE SKY.

I'D PREFER SOME FLAMES. BIG LEAF
PILE BONFIRES THAT MICHIGAN
KIDS COULD DANCE AROUND,
POSSESSED BY SPIRITS THAT
AREN'T SO GENTLE OR TAME. A
BIG BONFIRE IN EVERY BACKYARD,
AND MAYBE IT'D BE SUMMER
AGAIN. WE COULD STRIP DOWN TO
SHORT SLEEVES AND CUT-OFFS,
AND PRETEND THE FLOATING
EMBERS ARE FIREFLIES. WITH
ENOUGH DEAD LEAVES, THERE
COULD BE A SECOND SUMMER.
A SEASON THAT LASTS AS LONG
AS THE LEAF PILES BURN,
ALL DAY, THE SKY'S BEEN GRAY.
MATT WARNED ME ABOUT THIS.
MATT GREW UP IN HOWELL, A
LITTLE TOWN NOT FAR FROM

DETROIT THAT'S INFAMOUS FOR ONCE
BEING THE HOME OF THE GRAND
DRAGON OF THE MICHIGAN KKK.
MATT TOLD ME THAT THE SKY
CAN BE GRAY FOR MOST OF THE
WINTER. "THE MICHIGAN GRAY,"
HE CALLED IT. I TRY TO CONVINCE
MYSELF THAT THE SUN IS UP
THERE SOMEWHERE ABOVE THE
CLOUDS. IT DOESN'T WORK. I
DECIDE THAT CLOUDY-SKY PEOPLE —
PEOPLE WHO GREW UP IN SEATTLE
OR PORTLAND OR HERE IN
DETROIT — HAVE MORE FAITH THAN
THOSE OF US WHO GREW UP IN
SUNSHINE STATES. CLOUDY-SKY
PEOPLE ARE SUSTAINED BY AN
UNSHAKABLE BELIEF THAT ONE
DAY, IT'LL BE MAY AND THE SKY

WILL FINALLY CLEAR, WHICH IS
WAY MORE FAITH THAN I'VE GOT.
HIGHWAY 12 DUMPS ME ON THE
FREEWAY. I CAN BARELY SEE,
THANKS TO THE MIST KICKED UP
BY THE BIG RIGS THAT WOOSH
PAST ME, PEDALS TO THE
METAL AND HAMMERS DOWN.
I DRIVE ALONG, DETERMINED NOT
TO START DREAMING ABOUT SOME
OTHER PLACE. IT'S TRICKY, SO
INSTEAD, I PRETEND I'M ALREADY
SOME PLACE ELSE, AND THIS
PLACE IS WHAT I'M DREAMING
ABOUT. THIS VERY FREEWAY IN
THIS VERY CITY. IN THE SKY
ABOVE ME, A JUMBO JET
STRUGGLES UP THROUGH THE
CLOUDS. FULL OF DETROITERS

WHOSE FAITH HAS GROWN WEAK.
WHO NEED TO BREAK THROUGH
THE GRAY AND SEE SUNSHINE
AND BLUE SKIES, THE WAY
DOUBTING THOMAS HAD TO SEE
SOME NAIL HOLES BEFORE
HE'D BELIEVE.

CAMELBACK BRIDGE

YPSILANTI

THE TREE IN CAREY'S SIDE YARD
IS LOSING ALL ITS LEAVES. IT'S
NOT EVEN WINDY. THEY'RE JUST
FALLING OFF THE BRANCHES AND
PILING UP ON THE GROUND. IT'S
AN AWFUL THING TO WATCH.
A FEW MONTHS BACK, THOSE
SAME LEAVES WERE BRIGHT
GREEN AND BRAND-NEW. BACK
THEN, YOU COULD SLEEP WITH
THE WINDOWS OPEN AND LET
THE NIGHT PRESS GENTLY AGAINST
YOUR WINDOW SCREENS. JUST
A FLIMSY SCREEN BETWEEN
YOU AND THE WHOLE NIGHT.
NOW THE SCREENS ARE IN THE
BASEMENT, AND THE STORM
WINDOWS ARE SEALED SHUT.

BY TOMORROW, ALL THE LEAVES
WILL HAVE FALLEN OFF THE TREE
IN CAREY'S SIDE YARD. THEN
SHE'LL RAKE THEM UP, AND STUFF
THEM IN A BLACK PLASTIC BAG
WHICH SHE'LL DRAG TO THE
CURB FOR THE GARBAGE TRUCK
TO PICK UP.

I SPEND THE DAY IN DETROIT
LOOKING FOR A PLACE TO LIVE.
CORKTOWN. MEXICAN TOWN.
MAYBE MIDTOWN OR HAMTRAMCK.
NEW NEIGHBORHOODS, AND A
NEW SET OF NAMES FOR THE
SAME OLD IMPOSSIBLY HIGH
EXPECTATIONS. I'VE GOT SOME
CRITERIA IN MIND. THERE
SHOULD BE A DECENT CUP OF
COFFEE NOT TOO FAR AWAY, AND
THERE SHOULD BE TRAIN WHISTLES

AT NIGHT, AND A DOWNSTAIRS
NEIGHBOR WHO SEWS HER OWN
CLOTHES AND WHO SMILES AT
YOU WHEN YOU SEE HER IN THE
HALLWAY. BUT THESE ARE JUST
ROUGH GUIDELINES.

EVERY APARTMENT I LOOK AT IS A
CRIME SCENE. THE DOORS ARE
KICKED IN, OR THE LOCKS ARE
JIMMIED. INSIDE, THE WALLS
ARE STRATEGICALLY PAINTED.
NOT PAINTED ALL OVER, BUT IN
SPOTS. A LITTLE DAUB OF FRESH
WHITE PAINT SHAPED LIKE A
CIGARETTE BURN OR A BULLET
HOLE OR A BLOOD STAIN. THE
APARTMENTS ALL LOOK ABOUT
THE SAME, BUT WITH SMALL
DIFFERENCES: A DIFFERENT
PATTERN OF MOLD ON THE CEILING;

A DIFFERENT RHYTHM TO THE
WATER DRIPPING FROM THE
KITCHEN FAUCET. I CONSIDER
EACH APARTMENT FROM THE
PERSPECTIVE OF A TENANT WHO,
AFTER LIVING IN ONE OF THESE
PLACES FOR A WHILE, MIGHT
FIND HIMSELF WRITING A
SUICIDE NOTE ONE DAY. I
CONSIDER HOW THE WORDING
MIGHT DEPEND ON THESE MINOR
DETAILS AND, IN FACT, HOW
JUST THE RIGHT DETAILS
COULD MAKE THE DIFFERENCE
BETWEEN A NOTE THAT'S REALLY
SUCCESSFUL AND ONE THAT'S
MERELY COMPETENT.

CORKTOWN

ALL THE SUDDEN, I'M AN 80-YEAR-
OLD WIDOWER LIVING ALONE ON
THE SECOND FLOOR OF A TWO-
FLAT APARTMENT BUILDING.
THERE'S A RING OF BONE
WHITE FLORESCENT TUBING
SCREWED INTO A SOCKET ON
THE CEILING, AND A WALL
HEATER THAT WHEEZES LIKE
AN IRON LUNG. THE LINOLEUM
IN THE KITCHEN IS ASBESTOS
BLUE, AND THE WINDOW BLINDS
ARE COATED WITH A LAYER OF
STICKY BLACK GREASE. I FIGURE
THE GREASE IS WHAT KILLED
THE LAST TENANT, SOME GUY
WHO FRIED UP A PORK CHOP
EVERY NIGHT FOR DECADES. THE

GREASE IS ALL THAT'S LEFT OF
THOSE BACHELOR DINNERS AND
THE BACHELOR WHO ATE THEM.
MOST PEOPLE DESCRIBE THE
GHOST THAT HAUNTS THEIR
HOUSE AS WHITE AND TRANS-
PARENT, BUT THE GHOST IN MY
APARTMENT IS A GREASY BLACK
GOO THAT COVERS EVERYTHING.

CHICAGO
MILWAUKEE @ PAULINA ST.

RECIPE FOR FAKE CHICKEN SALAD.

I LIVE ALONE IN THIS <u>APARTMENT</u> IN DETROIT.

HI, BILL.

I SHARE AN ENTRY-WAY WITH MY DOWNSTAIRS NEIGHBORS. WHEN THE ENTRYWAY SMELLS LIKE CIGARETTE SMOKE AND SPICY MEN'S COLOGNE, I KNOW MY NEIGHBORS ARE HOME. THERE ARE TWO OF THEM: A FRIENDLY TAN GUY WHO LEAVES HIS DOOR OPEN AND SAYS HI WHEN I COME HOME, AND AN UNFRIENDLY GUY WITH GLASSES WHO

DOESN'T. THE GUYS DON'T ACTUALLY LIVE THERE. THEY USE THE APARTMENT AS AN OFFICE. I FIND OUT FROM ANOTHER NEIGHBOR WHAT THESE GUYS DO. THEY'RE BOOKIES. THE NEIGHBOR WHO TELLS ME THIS REFERS TO THEM AS "THE MOBSTERS."

"THE PATTERN"

THE LINOLEUM FLOOR IN MY KITCHEN IS A DREAMY FADED BLUE THAT I DECIDE IS THE COLOR OF LIVING ALONE IN DETROIT. AT NIGHT, UNDER THE 60-WATT LIGHTBULB HANGING FROM THE CEILING, IT'S THE COLOR YOU SEE WHEN YOU STICK YOUR HEAD IN THE OVEN AND TURN ON THE GAS.

LATELY WHEN I GET HOME, I'VE
BEEN MAKING FAKE CHICKEN
SALAD. IT'S PRETTY EASY.

 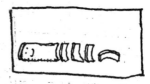

1. FIRST, DICE UP
SOME RED
ONION.

2. THEN CHOP UP A
COUPLE STICKS
OF CELERY.

3. THROW THE ONIONS
AND CELERY AND A
FISTFUL OF CRUMBLED
PECANS INTO A BOWL.
THEN GRAB SOME
FAKE MAYO: NAYONAISE OR
VEGANAISE. I DON'T THINK THIS
STUFF IS HEALTHY, BUT WHAT
CAN YOU DO? HEAVE A COUPLE
BIG DOLLOPS OF FAKE MAYO INTO
THE BOWL.

NOW ABOUT THE (FAKE) CHICKEN. YOU CAN USE WHATEVER YOU LIKE. I MEAN, I DON'T CARE. ME, I PREFER THE WHITE WAVE "STIR FRY STRIPS."☆

☆ THIS IS NOT AN ENDORSEMENT OF WHITE WAVE☆ PRODUCTS.

☆ CONFIDENTIAL TO WHITE WAVE: I'LL TOTALLY ENDORSE YOUR PRODUCTS! PLEASE SEND FREE SAMPLES TO THE P.O. BOX LISTED ON THE BACK COVER.

EEEEEEEEE!

FRY UP THE "CHICKEN" TILL THE SMOKE ALARM GOES OFF.

THEN TOSS IT IN THE BOWL WITH THE REST OF THE STUFF. ADD SOME PEPPER AND A DASH OF SOY SAUCE. I LIKE A COUPLE SHAKES OF CAYENNE PEPPER, TOO. THEN MIX IT ALL UP!

NOW IT'S TIME TO MAKE A SANDWICH! SLOP A SUPER-SIZED SCOOP OF "CHICKEN" SALAD ON SOME BREAD.

ADD TOMATOES, AND AVOCADO IF YOU CAN AFFORD IT.

LATELY, AVOCADOS HAVE BEEN RUNNING $2 A PIECE. THEN POP OPEN A BOTTLE OF BELL'S AMBER ALE☆ AND DIG IN.

☆ CONFIDENTIAL TO BELL'S BEER CORPORATION: PLEASE SEE CONFIDENTIAL TO WHITE WAVE.

CRITICAL MASS

THE FIRST TIME I RIDE, IT'S JANUARY AND IT'S COLD. THERE'S JUST THREE OF US: ME AND THE TWO GUYS WHO RUN THE DETROIT CRITICAL MASS WEB SITE. AFTER A FEW BLOCKS, OUR FACES ARE FROZEN AND IT'S HARD TO TALK WITHOUT SLURRING OUR WORDS. "ISS COL'" ONE OF THE GUYS SAYS. "ISS LIKE AR' BAH-IES ARE STAR-ING TO DIE," THE OTHER ONE SAYS. WE DECIDE TO CALL IT QUITS AND GET SOME HOT CHOCOLATE INSTEAD.

THE SECOND TIME I RIDE, IT'S AUGUST AND IT'S NICE. THIS TIME, THERE ARE FIFTEEN OF US, AND WE GO ON A LONG RIDE: ALL THE WAY TO BELLE ISLE, THEN UP TO HEIDELBERG

DETROIT

DOWN IN ARIZONA, YOU CROSS THE
BORDER TO BUY CHEAP PHAR-
MACEUTICALS IN MEXICO. UP
HERE IN DETROIT, YOU CROSS
INTO CANADA FOR CUT-RATE
LASIK EYE SURGERY. TO GET
FROM DETROIT TO WINDSOR,
ONTARIO, YOU HAVE TO CROSS
THE DETROIT RIVER (WHICH,
FOR YOU GEOGRAPHY BUFFS, ISN'T
A RIVER BUT A STRAIT;
WHICH, FOR YOU LANGUAGE BUFFS,
IS THE ENGLISH TRANSLATION
OF THE FRENCH WORD "DÉTROIT";
WHICH, FOR YOU HISTORY BUFFS,
IS HOW THE CITY GOT ITS
NAME). YOU CAN CROSS THE
DETROIT RIVER THROUGH A
TUNNEL OR ON A SUSPENSION

DETROIT

DOWN IN ARIZONA, YOU CROSS THE
BORDER TO BUY CHEAP PHAR-
MACEUTICALS IN MEXICO. UP
HERE IN DETROIT, YOU CROSS
INTO CANADA FOR CUT-RATE
LASIK EYE SURGERY. TO GET
FROM DETROIT TO WINDSOR,
ONTARIO, YOU HAVE TO CROSS
THE DETROIT RIVER (WHICH,
FOR YOU GEOGRAPHY BUFFS, ISN'T
A RIVER BUT A STRAIT;
WHICH, FOR YOU LANGUAGE BUFFS,
IS THE ENGLISH TRANSLATION
OF THE FRENCH WORD "DÉTROIT";
WHICH, FOR YOU HISTORY BUFFS,
IS HOW THE CITY GOT ITS
NAME). YOU CAN CROSS THE
DETROIT RIVER THROUGH A
TUNNEL OR ON A SUSPENSION

BRIDGE. I CAN'T THINK OF A SINGLE GOOD REASON NOT TO USE THE BRIDGE. IT'S CALLED THE AMBASSADOR, AND IT WAS BUILT IN 1930, AROUND THE TIME ALL THOSE FAMOUS BRIDGES WERE BEING BUILT OUT IN SAN FRANCISCO. IF I STAND IN THE FAR CORNER OF MY APARTMENT, I CAN SORT OF SEE THE BRIDGE OUT MY FRONT WINDOW. AT FIRST, I CONSIDERED CRAMMING ALL MY STUFF IN THAT CORNER: MY AIR MATTRESS AND MY ROLLER CHAIR AND THE BIG, HEAVY TABLE I BORROWED FROM MY PARENTS' GARAGE. BUT IT JUST WASN'T PRACTICAL.

I LIVE UPSTAIRS IN A 2-FLAT. TWO OLDER GUYS RUN SOME KIND OF BUSINESS OUT OF THE

APARTMENT BELOW MINE. I HAVE
NEIGHBORS WHO LIVE IN THE
APARTMENTS ALL AROUND ME,
BUT I RARELY SEE THEM AND
NEVER HEAR THEM. NO TV
NOISE OR LATE-NIGHT YELLING
MATCHES. NO DRUNKEN PARTIES.
IT'S SO QUIET THAT I TRY TO BE
QUIET, TOO. WALKING SOFTLY.
KEEPING MY VOICE DOWN WHEN
I TALK ON THE PHONE. THE
QUIET MAKES ME PARANOID. LIKE
ALL MY NEIGHBORS ARE LISTENING
TO ME. LEANING WITH THEIR
EARS AGAINST THE WALLS. HOLD-
ING THEIR BREATH AND LISTEN-
ING CLOSE.
I LIVE ON A STREET THAT IS PITCH
DARK BECAUSE THE STREETLIGHTS
ARE OUT. SOMEONE TELLS ME

IT'S BECAUSE THE STREETLIGHTS
IN DETROIT ARE ANTIQUES AND
IT'S HARD TO FIND REPLACEMENT
PARTS. SOMEONE ELSE TELLS
ME THAT SCAVENGERS PULL THE
COPPER WIRES OUT OF THE
LIGHTS AND SELL THEM FOR
SCRAP. SCAVENGERS PREY ON
CITIES WHEN THEY'RE DOWN
THE WAY OPPORTUNISTIC IN-
FECTIONS AFFLICT PEOPLE WHOSE
IMMUNE SYSTEMS ARE WEAK.
ORDINARILY, A CITY CAN FIGHT
THEM OFF, BUT WHEN TIMES GET
TOUGH, THEY TAKE OVER. BACK
IN THE EARLY 1980's, WHEN NEW
YORK WAS GOING THROUGH ITS
OWN TOUGH TIMES, SCAVENGERS
STOLE SO MUCH COPPER WIRE
OUT OF THE SUBWAY THAT ONE
SUMMER DAY, THE SYSTEM

OVERLOADED AND THE TRAINS GROUND TO A STOP. HERE IN DETROIT, ON MY STREET, THE SCAVENGERS HAVE KNOCKED OUT THE STREETLIGHTS. PART OF ME THINKS THE SCAVENGERS SUCK, AND PART OF ME IS HAPPY THAT I CAN WALK OUT MY FRONT DOOR AND LOOK UP AND SEE THE STARS.

THERE'S A HIPPY BAKERY IN MIDTOWN, NEAR THE UNIVERSITY, ONE MORNING, I GO THERE WITH MY FRIEND DAVID. DETROIT ISN'T A HIPPY BAKERY KIND OF TOWN, WHICH MAKES THE PLACE FEEL IMPROBABLE AND EXCITING. WE TALK ABOUT THE CITY, AND THE SUBURBS WHERE THE CITY HAS GONE — HALF OF IT, ANYWAY.

DETROIT USED TO BE A CITY OF TWO MILLION BACK IN THE 50's. NOW THERE'S LESS THAN A MILLION, AND THE CITY IS STILL SHRINKING. WE TALK ABOUT THE GRID, HOW IT MOVES ACROSS THE FACE OF THE EARTH, FIRST AS AN IDEA, AND THEN AS TRACT HOUSES AND STRIP MALLS SET IN NEAT ROWS. SOMETIMES I WONDER IF THE OLD WORLD ISN'T STILL THERE, UNDERNEATH THE HATCH LINES OF ENLIGHTENED REASON. THAT OLD, MAGIC WORLD THAT HAUNTS US, THE WAY THE RESTLESS DEAD HAUNT MODEL HOMES BUILT ON TOP OF INDIAN BURIAL GROUNDS.

DETROIT — The city has begun a new effort to protect its street lamps from vandalism and scrap-seekers, but city officials admit it won't protect the poles from the biggest problem they face: age.

Over the past few weeks, Detroit crews have been slipping plastic barrel-shaped covers over street lamp poles along Jefferson Avenue as part of a $1.2 million project to prevent scrappers and vandals from pulling off metal covers.

The "shroud" project calls for covering 21,000 of the city's more than 85,000 wood and metal street light poles by the end of the year, according to Al Fields, deputy chief operating officer for the city of Detroit.

Street lighting consistently is the No. 1 concern of residents who fear that some 9,000 lights that don't work make the neighborhoods less safe. One out of every four complaints to the ombudsman's office are related to the lighting department.

The shrouds are just a small part of Mayor Kwame Kilpatrick's efforts to address the city's antiquated lighting before the 2006 Super Bowl and other high profile events.

In a 300-year-old city, Fields said original fixtures and wiring can still be found in city lights.

"There are so many different issues with lighting," Fields said. "Some of (the wiring) has been pulled out to cause it to go bad. Some of it is the old infrastructure, circuits need to be replaced. It's hardly ever just a bulb."

The city is currently trying to fix 5,000 of the estimated 9,000 broken lights by the end of the year. The shrouds prevent people from tampering with the lights and poles.

The city hired T&B Conveyor Products, a local, minority-owned business to design the shrouds — a plastic cover made from the same material as some car fenders — and install them. They are meant to prevent people from tampering with the base of the lights.

"It's hard to take off," Fields said. So far, only one shroud has been damaged and that was because a car ran into the light fixture, he said.

Michael Kidd, general manager of T&B, said two crews have installed most shrouds along Jefferson. They are now placing the shrouds on downtown street lamp poles and will eventually include other light-deprived communities.

"We've been working with the city for about two years to come up with a design that's cost effective and esthetically pleasing and to enhance safety," Kidd said. The company has a patent pending on the shroud.

THE DEQUINDRE CUT IS AN
OPEN TRENCH THAT
FREIGHT TRAINS USED TO
ROLL THROUGH. IT WAS
BUILT BACK IN THE 1920's
BY THE GRAND TRUNK WESTERN
R.R. AND CUT THROUGH THE
INDUSTRIAL DISTRICT ON
DETROIT'S NEAR EAST SIDE. IT'S
ABOUT 30 FEET BELOW GRADE.
PEOPLE DRIVE OVER IT ALL THE
TIME BUT PROBABLY DON'T EVEN
NOTICE. NOW THAT THE TRAINS
ARE GONE, THE CUT BELONGS TO
HOMELESS GUYS AND GRAFFITI
ARTISTS. IN THE SPRING, THE
CUT IS FULL OF TALL GRASS AND
GHETTO PALMS. IF YOU EVER
WONDERED WHAT THE END OF
CIVILIZATION LOOKS LIKE, IT
LOOKS LIKE THIS: A BIG CITY
FREIGHT RAILROAD THAT'S
BECOME A NATURE PRESERVE.

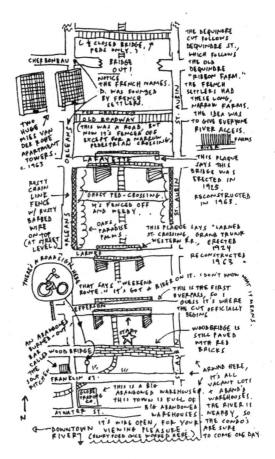

THE DEQUINDRE CUT FOLLOWS DEQUINDRE ST., WHICH FOLLOWS THE OLD DEQUINDRE "RIBBON FARM." THE FRENCH SETTLERS HAD THESE LONG, NARROW FARMS. THE IDEA WAS TO GIVE EVERYONE RIVER ACCESS.

FARMS

CHERBONNEAU

(½ CLOSED BRIDGE, PEDS ONLY.)

BRIDGE OUT!

NOTICE THE FRENCH NAMES. D. WAS FOUNDED BY FRENCH SETTLERS.

AUBIN ST.

TWO HUGE MIES VAN DER ROHE APARTMENT TOWERS. c. 1963

OLD ROADWAY
(THIS WAS A ROAD, BUT NOW IT'S FENCED OFF EXCEPT FOR A NARROW PEDESTRIAN CROSSING)

LAFAYETTE

ORLEANS ST.

RUSTY CHAIN LINK FENCE W/ RUSTY BARBED WIRE ON TOP (AT STREET LEVELS)

GHOST PED-CROSSING. IT'S FENCED OFF AND WEEDY

ST. AUBIN

THIS PLAQUE SAYS THIS BRIDGE WAS ERECTED IN 1925. RECONSTRUCTED IN 1963.

OAKS PARADISE FARMS

THIS PLAQUE SAYS "LARNED ST. CROSSING, GRAND TRUNK WESTERN R.R., ERECTED 1924 RECONSTRUCTED 1963

LARNED

THERE'S A ROAD SIGN HERE

THAT SAYS "WEEKEND ROUTE." IT'S GOT A BIKER ON IT. I DON'T KNOW WHAT IT MEANS.

THIS IS THE FIRST OVERPASS, SO I GUESS IT'S WHERE THE CUT OFFICIALLY BEGINS

JEFFERSON

START

WOODBRIDGE IS STILL PAVED WITH RED BRICKS

AN ABANDONED BURNED-OUT BAR CALLED THE SOUP KITCHEN

WOOD BRIDGE

FRANKLIN ST.

GLOBE TRADING CO.

ATWATER ST.

N

THIS IS A BIG ABANDONED WAREHOUSE. THIS TOWN IS FULL OF BIG ABANDONED WAREHOUSES. IT'S WIDE OPEN, FOR YOUR VIEWING PLEASURE (HENRY FORD ONCE WORKED HERE.)

AROUND HERE, IT'S ALL VACANT LOTS & ABAND'D WAREHOUSES. THE RIVER IS NEARBY, SO THE CONDOS ARE SURE TO COME ONE DAY

← DOWNTOWN RIVER →

321

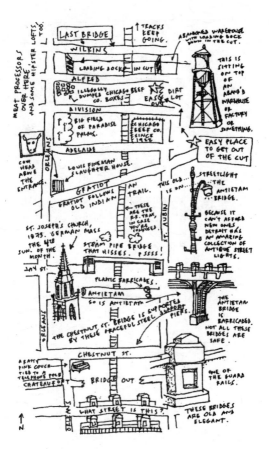

LAST BRIDGE

↑ TRACKS KEEP GOING.

WILKINS

ABANDONED WAREHOUSE WITH LOADING DOCK DOWN IN THE CUT.

LOADING DOCKS IN CUT

MEAT PROCESSORS OVER HERE AND SOME HIPSTER LOFTS.

THIS IS SITTING ON TOP OF AN ABAND'D WAREHOUSE OR FACTORY OR SOMETHING.

ALFRED

ILLEGALLY DUMPED CHICAGO BEEF CO. BOXES.

★ DIRT EASY LOT OUT

DIVISION

ORLEANS

BIG FIELD OF PARADISE PALMS.

CHICAGO BEEF CO. SINCE 1952

ADELAIDE

COW HEAD ABOVE THE ENTRANCE.

LOUIS FINEMAN SLAUGHTER HOUSE.

★ EASY PLACE TO GET OUT OF THE CUT

GRATIOT

GRATIOT FOLLOWS AN OLD INDIAN TRAIL.

THIS OLD ── STREETLIGHT

··· IS ON··· THE ANTIETAM BRIDGE.

← THESE ARE THE R.R. TRAX, IN CASE YOU'RE CONFUSED.

ST. AUBIN

BECAUSE IT CAN'T AFFORD NEW ONES DETROIT HAS AN AMAZING COLLECTION OF ANTIQUE STREET LIGHTS.

ST. JOSEPH'S CHURCH, 1873. GERMAN MASS THE 4TH SUN. OF THE MONTH.

JAY ST.

STEAM PIPE BRIDGE THAT HISSES. PSSSS!

PLASTIC BARRICADES.

ANTIETAM

SO IS ANTIETAM.

THE CHESTNUT ST. BRIDGE IS SUPPORTED BY THESE GRACEFUL STEEL SUPPORT PIERS.

ORLEANS

THE ANTIETAM BRIDGE IS BARRICADED. NOT ALL THESE BRIDGES ARE SAFE.

CHESTNUT ST.

A PRETTY PINK COUCH TIED TO A TELEPHONE POLE

CHATEAUFORT

BRIDGE OUT

ONE OF THE GUARD RAILS.

↑ N

WHAT STREET IS THIS?

THESE BRIDGES ARE OLD AND ELEGANT.

322

BELLE ISLE

THERE ARE PALM TREES IN THE
MIDDLE OF THE DETROIT RIVER.
CACTUSES, TOO. THEY'RE IN THE
CONSERVATORY OUT ON BELLE ISLE.
THE CONSERVATORY IS OLD; A
STEEL AND GLASS GREENHOUSE
BUILT IN 1904. WHEN I WALK
IN, IT'S HOT AND THE AIR IS
HEAVY AND MY GLASSES FOG
OVER, WHICH SEEMS LIKE THE
KIND OF THING THAT SHOULD
HAPPEN; THE WAY THE IMAGE
FOGS OVER IN THE MOVIES TO
LET YOU KNOW YOU'RE LEAVING
THIS WORLD AND ENTERING
ANOTHER ONE: A DREAM; A
FLASHBACK; THE PAST. WHEN
I CAN FINALLY SEE AGAIN, I'M
STANDING UNDER THE DATE

PALMS, AND I'M SURROUNDED BY THE GEARS AND PULLEYS THAT OPEN THE WINDOWS, AND THE PRESSURE GAUGES AND PIPES OF THE RADIATOR SYSTEM. THE PLACE LOOKS LIKE AN ART NOUVEAU TIME MACHINE PILOTED BY BOTANIST TIME TRAVELERS. THEY'VE COME FROM THE YEAR 1904, BUT THEY DIDN'T COUNT ON THE FACT THAT AS THEY MOVED THROUGH TIME, THEIR TIME MACHINE WOULD AGE AND RUST AND FALL APART, STRAND-ING THEM HERE IN OUR TIME.

THE VOLUNTEER WHO TAKES CARE OF THE ORCHID ROOM NOTICES I'M CARRYING A BIKE HELMET. HE TELLS ME HE'S A BIKE RIDER, AND HE USED TO WEAR A HELMET,

TOO, BUT HE DOESN'T ANYMORE.
THE GUY TELLS ME HE LIVES
IN A NEIGHBORHOOD CALLED
INDIAN VILLAGE. IT USED TO BE
REALLY FANCY, THEN IT, LIKE
THE REST OF DETROIT, FELL ON
HARD TIMES AND HE WAS
ABLE TO BUY AN OLD MANSION
FOR NEXT TO NOTHING. NOT
LONG AFTER HE MOVED IN, HE
WAS WALKING HIS DOG ONE
NIGHT. SOME KIDS CAME UP TO
HIM ON THE STREET AND
DEMANDED HIS MONEY. THE
GUY STARTED RUNNING, SO THE
KIDS SHOT HIM. THEY SHOT HIS
DOG, TOO. THE GUY AND HIS DOG
RECOVERED, BUT AFTER THAT,
HE STOPPED WEARING A BIKE
HELMET.

St. Patrick's Day

THE PARADE IS SUPPOSED TO PASS
BY ON MICHIGAN AVENUE WHICH
IS PRETTY CLOSE TO WHERE I LIVE,
SO I DECIDE TO CHECK IT OUT.
MICHIGAN AVE. IS ONE OF THE
BIG BOULEVARDS THAT POKE
LIKE SPOKES OUT OF DOWNTOWN'S
HUB. THE RADIAL ROADS DATE TO
THE EARLY 1800's AND A GOVERNOR
NAMED CASS. LATER, THOSE
STREETS WOULD REMIND PEOPLE
OF THE GRAND BOULEVARDS
HAUSMANN BUILT IN PARIS IN
THE 1860's. DETROIT WAS SOME-
TIMES CALLED "THE PARIS OF
THE MIDWEST." SOME PEOPLE
STILL CALL IT THAT, BUT ONLY
WHEN THEY'RE TRYING TO BE
FUNNY. MICHIGAN AVENUE AND

GRAND RIVER AND WOODWARD AND
GRATIOT, ROADS THAT LAUNCH
OUT OF DOWNTOWN AT DIAGONALS
AND SMACK INTO THE CITY'S
STREET GRID THE WAY ALPHA
PARTICLES SMACK INTO OUR
CELLS, CUTTING A HOLE
THROUGH THE STUFF WE'RE MADE
OUT OF; THE BORING GRID
SYSTEM OF OUR DNA.

I LIVE JUST OFF OF MICHIGAN AVE.
NEAR THE OLD, EMPTY TIGER'S
STADIUM. THERE'S A ROW OF
IRISH BARS THAT SOMEHOW HANG
ON EVEN THOUGH THE STADIUM
CLOSED DOWN YEARS AGO:
CASEY'S AND McCARTHY'S AND
O'BLIVION'S. THE OLD PATRONS
STILL COME AROUND, EVEN THOUGH
THEY LIVE OUT IN THE SUBURBS

NOW, ALONG I-94 AND I-96 AND
I-75. THE FREEWAYS BYPASSED
THE OLD BOULEVARDS. AND AS
DETROIT FELL APART, EVERYBODY
WHO COULD AFFORD IT HOPPED IN
THEIR CAR AND SPED TO A NEW
LIFE BEYOND THE CITY LIMITS --
OR MAYBE IT'S THE OTHER WAY
AROUND. ON ST. PATRICK'S DAY,
THOSE PEOPLE DRIVE BACK INTO
THE CITY THEY ABANDONED AND
THEY MARCH DOWN THE MIDDLE
OF MICHIGAN AVENUE BEHIND
BANNERS THAT SAY "THE
ANCIENT ORDER OF HIBERNIANS,"
OR "THE FRIENDLY ORDER OF
ST. PATRICK." THE PARADE AL-
TERNATES BETWEEN WHITE IRISH
PEOPLE FROM THE SUBURBS AND

BLACK HIGH SCHOOL MARCHING
BANDS FROM DETROIT. WATCHING
THE PARADE IS LIKE WATCHING
A HUGE PERFORMANCE ART
SPECTACLE ABOUT RACE IN THIS
CITY. A GROUP OF ANCIENT
HIBERNIANS TODDLES BY, TIPSY
AND TOSSING GREEN BEADS AND
TOOTSIE ROLLS. THEN COMES THE
HENRY FORD HIGH SCHOOL MARCHING
BAND, ALL LOOSE-LIMBED AND
COOL, WACKING THE STUFFING
OUT OF THEIR BASS DRUMS.
THE PARADE LASTS FOREVER, AND
THERE'S NOTHING FANCY ABOUT
IT. NO CORPORATE FLOATS OR
GIANT CARTOON BALLOONS. IT'S
AN OLD-SCHOOL WORKING CLASS
PARADE. I KEEP GETTING CHOKED
UP, BECAUSE MICHIGAN AVENUE

ISN'T REALLY LIKE THIS. LIVELY
AND ALIVE. IT'S A FALSE LIFE,
WHICH MAKES THE CITY AS IT
REALLY IS — THE CITY IT'LL BE
AGAIN IN A COUPLE HOURS - ALL
THE SADDER. EVEN THE DETROIT
COPS LINING THE PARADE ROUTE
ARE IN A GOOD MOOD. SMILING
AND LAUGHING. MAYBE BECAUSE
TODAY, THEY FEEL LIKE REAL
COPS IN A REAL CITY. OR MAYBE
BECAUSE CROWD CONTROL IS A
NOVELTY IN A CITY WITHOUT
CROWDS.

YOU WILL NEVER NEED
TO WORRY ABOUT
A STEADY INCOME.
1 23 26 36 39, 23

BIKE FERRY!

YOU CAN GET TO CANADA FROM
DETROIT BY BRIDGE OR BY
TUNNEL, BUT NOT BY BIKE. THE
BRIDGE AND TUNNEL ARE FOR
CARS AND TRUCKS. PERIOD.

CANADA IS CLOSE,
JUST ACROSS THE
RIVER, SO IT SEEMS
UNFAIR THAT YOU
CAN'T JUST PEDAL
OVER THERE.

THEN, AT A CRITICAL MASS RIDE, I HEAR A RUMOR...

THERE'S A TRUCK FERRY...

GET ON BOARD!

DETROIT - WINDSOR
TRUCK FERRY

DEPARTS

DETROIT	WINDSOR
7:00am	8:00am
9:00am	10:00am
11:00am	12:00pm
1:00pm	2:00pm
3:00pm	4:00pm

TURNS OUT IT'S TRUE. I CALL THEM UP.

"DO YOU TAKE BIKES?" I ASK.

THERE'S A PAUSE.

LIKE MAYBE THIS ISN'T A QUESTION THE GUY GETS EVERYDAY.

"YEAH," HE FINALLY SAYS.

"HOW MUCH IS IT?" I ASK.

ANOTHER PAUSE. "TWO BUCKS."

THE FERRY TERMINAL IS DOWN
RIVER, IN THE SMOKY, STINKY
INDUSTRIAL WASTELAND NEAR
ZUG ISLAND. THE OFFICE IS IN
A LITTLE STEEL-SIDED
BUILDING. I BUY A TICKET. A
FRIENDLY BORDER COP COMES
OUT AND ASKS ME SOME QUESTIONS:

WHERE ARE
YOU FROM?

I'M FROM
HERE.

HERE?! YOU MEAN
RIGHT HERE
IN

I MEAN HERE
IN DETROIT.

THIS PARKING
LOT?!

SORRY, YOU NEED A VISA TO GET IN.

WHILE I'M WAITING FOR THE FERRY TO BOARD, I CONSOLE MYSELF WITH THOUGHTS OF WHAT HAPPENS TO BORDER COPS WHEN THEY APPROACH THE PEARLY GATES.

THE FERRY, IT TURNS OUT, IS A TUG BOAT WITH A BARGE LASHED TO IT.

I ROLL ABOARD JUST AHEAD OF A TANKER TRUCK.

INSTEAD OF CUTTING STRAIGHT
ACROSS THE RIVER, WE FLOAT
DOWNSTREAM, PAST THE BIG
STEEL MILL ON ZUG ISLAND,
AND PAST THE OLD BOB-LO
ISLAND FERRY ANCHORED NEAR
THE MOUTH OF THE ROUGE RIVER.

THE FERRY IS CALLED THE
STE. CLAIRE. IT'S ALMOST 100
YEARS OLD. DURING THE
SUMMER, IT USED TO CARRY

DETROITERS TO THE
AMUSEMENT PARK ON BOB-LO
ISLAND. BUT THE PARK
CLOSED OVER A DECADE AGO,
AND NO ONE'S SURE WHAT TO
DO WITH THE OLD FERRY. THE
CURRENT OWNER OPENED IT
AS A HAUNTED HOUSE LAST
HALLOWEEN. HE CALLED IT
"THE NAUTICAL NIGHTMARE."
MEANWHILE, THE FERRY I'M ON
DOCKS PRETTY
FAR DOWN
RIVER FROM
WINDSOR, IN

AN INDUSTRIAL PARK THAT'S
MORE PARK THAN INDUSTRY.
I ROLL ONTO A GRAVEL
PARKING LOT AND CHECK IN
AT THE BORDER SHACK. THERE'S
ONE BORDER COP INSIDE. SHE
TELLS ME TO HAVE A NICE RIDE.

Index